MY CHILD...SURVEY THE WONDROUS CROSS

MY CHILD... SURVEY THE WONDROUS CROSS

----o----

The Message of the Cross
Is the Power of God

----o----

PAUL CUMMINGS

----o----

MY CHILD... SURVEY THE WONDROUS CROSS

The Message of the Cross Is the Power of God

----o----

----o----

Copyright ©2025 Paul Cummings

----o----

Published by Paul Cummings

----o----

PO Box 535 – Turramurra – NSW – 2074 – Australia

----o----

All rights reserved. No portion of this book may be reproduced, stored in a retrieval system, or transmitted in any form or by any means – electronic, mechanical, photocopy, recording, or any other – except for brief quotations in printed reviews, without prior written permission of the publisher. Write: Permissions, Paul Cummings, PO Box 535, Turramurra, NSW 2074, Australia.

----o----

Digital Online ISBN: 978-1-7637298-6-5

Paperback ISBN: 978-1-7637298-7-2

----o----

All Scripture quotations, unless otherwise indicated, are taken from the Holy Bible, New International Version®, NIV®. Copyright ©1973, 1978, 1984, 2011 by Biblica, Inc.™ Used by permission of Zondervan. All rights reserved worldwide. www.zondervan.com The "NIV" and "New International Version" are trademarks registered in the United States Patent and Trademark Office by Biblica, Inc.™

INTRODUCTION

For many people the Cross of Jesus is a symbol or a type of logo of the Christian faith. By wearing a cross around their neck some think it proves they are a Christian. Amongst other things, some believe it can protect them from evil. The image of a cross can be a great reminder of what Christ has done for us. The truth is that the cross is far much more than a symbol of remembrance. In reality, working together with the Holy Spirit, it is a source of power in a Christian's daily life.

Living by the principles of the cross leads to a transformation in a Christian's life. The cross should be foundational teaching for every believer in Christ. Far from being only a once off event all those years ago, it can impact lives today in powerful ways. The cross was the means to the death and resurrection of Jesus. In the life of a Christian, it is still the means of death and resurrection from an old life to a new one.

In scripture faith is the belief in things unseen (Hebrews 11:1) and we are to walk by faith. So we are to takes steps of faith based not on what we can see but on what we cannot see. This means that what we choose to believe is of primary and fundamental importance.

To believe in the cross is to believe the crucifixion of Jesus actually happened. Which of course is important to becoming a Christian. But to believe in the cross also calls us to walk in the victory Christ has won for us by the cross. I for one am always learning of the glorious cross of Christ.

This book is a collection of readings written in the first person as if Father God is speaking to us in a devotional way. I do not claim that what is written is a direct revelation from God like the Bible is. I have taken Bible verses and given insights to the verse in an attempt to open up sound Biblical doctrine to the everyday person without necessarily knowing they are learning doctrine. Every reading relates in some way to the cross and what it has achieved. My aim is to introduce doctrines of the cross without complicated theological jargon. My greater aim is that a person will read, learn, prayerfully seek the Lord on the issues raised, and walk in the victory of the cross.

Your servant in Christ,

Paul

Item index – Item number not page number.

1. Separated by Sin
2. I Am Holy
3. Unkeepable Law
4. Two Fatherhoods
5. Slavery to Satan
6. Spiritual Death
7. Wall of Separation
8. Communication breakdown
9. Being Found
10. Way to Forgiveness
11. Perfect Sacrifice
12. Prophetic Guidance
13. Two Adams
14. Jesus the Mediator
15. Jesus the Priest
16. Jesus the Redeemer

17. Jesus the God Man
18. Why the Cross?
19. Wrath of God
20. Wrath Removed
21. Certificate of Debt
22. Forsaken
23. It Is Finished
24. Freedom From Slavery
25. Qualified Redeemer
26. Jesus the Gift
27. Substitutionary Death
28. One Lamb For Few
29. One Goat All Israel
30. The Ultimate Lamb
31. Reconciliation
32. No Hostility
33. Justification
34. By Faith

35. No Confidence

36. Peace

37. No Condemnation

38. Me For You

39. The Accuser

40. Total Forgiveness

41. Forgiveness Too

42. Focus

43. Baptism into Death

44. Penalty and Power

45. The Law and Satan

46. Freedom Without Lawlessness

47. Ultimate Freedom

48. Guilt Trips

49. Freedom to Serve

50. Regenerate

51. Listening Renovation

52. Points of View

53. Fairh Intimacy

54. Self-Centred to Christ-Centred

55. Claim the Victory

56. Best Plan

57. Bear Fruit

58. New Position

59. Blessings

60. Oneness

61. Spiritual Bankrupt

62. Adam to Christ

63. Don't Punish Yourself

64. Focus on the Son not the Sin

65. Unworthy

66. Beautiful Feet

67. Accepted or Rejected Gift

68. Do Not Add or Take Away

69. Cheap Grace

70. Faith Response

71. Faith Plus Repentance?

72. Faith Plus Baptism?

73. Cross of Paradise

74. Take Up Your Cross

75. Misunderstood Cross

76. Cross of Power and Wisdom

77. Who Put My Son on the Cross?

78. Don't be an Enemy of the Cross

79. Set Apart

80. Don't Forget

1.

SEPARATED BY SIN

My Child ...

Sin has put a barrier between myself and my creation. It cannot be removed by a person's own efforts. Such is the alienation it has brought. Look around the world and see the destruction sin has brought on every level. Each person needs to recognise the reality of sin. Not only the sin of others but their own personal sin. I want you to recognise your own personal sin. I want you to recognise your own personal sin and to take responsibility for it. Examine yourself against my word, the Bible. Look at your moral life in the light of my Word. Think of your personal struggles and sufferings. Consider your anxiousness and unhealthy desires. It should not be difficult to recognise sin in your life. This is the human dilemma. Sin is at the root of all sorrows. People are sinners and need forgiveness and reconciliation to me their heavenly Father. As large a barrier that sin is between me and my creation, it can be removed. Sin has taken people captive. But there is an everlasting solution to it. What seems an immoveable barrier between you and I can be removed. It is the way of the cross. What you are not able to do yourself my Son has done for you. All by the power of the cross. Examine yourself.

----o----

....for all have sinned and fall short of the glory of God, [24] and all are justified freely by his grace through the redemption that came by Christ Jesus. Romans 3:23-24

2.

I AM HOLY

My Child . . .

I am holy. I am perfect. No human's character can measure up to mine. My Holy character is an obstacle that has to be removed for a person to have fellowship with me. This is because to be accepted by me a person needs to become perfect and holy too. I will always be Holy so it is not me that needs to be changed. No person can achieve this of themselves. It is an impossible standard. Only I can make it possible. Only I can bestow holiness and perfection on a person. True fellowship with me was lost in the Garden of Eden by Adam. Restored fellowship with me is now possible through another man, my Son, Jesus. One man lost the fellowship and another paved the way to restore it. The only way for a person to become holy and acceptable by me is through the cross. You have been reconciled to me. You have been made Holy. We can have fellowship. You are now a member of my family. I am your Father. You are my child. And all because of the work of my Son on the cross making you Holy.

----o----

For if, by the trespass of the one man, death reigned through that one man, how much more will those who receive God's abundant provision of grace and of the gift of righteousness reign in life through the one man, Jesus Christ! [18] Consequently, just as one trespass resulted in condemnation for all people, so also one righteous act resulted in justification and life for all people. [19] For just as through the disobedience of the one man the many were made sinners, so also through the obedience of the one man the many will be made righteous. Romans 5:17-19

----o----

To all in Rome who are loved by God and called to be his holy people: Grace and peace to you from God our Father and from the Lord Jesus Christ. Romans 1:7

----o----

3.

UNKEEPABLE LAW

My Child . . .

The obstacles of sin and my holy character are not the only obstacles that separate me from my creation. Together with these you also need to understand the barrier of my law. The laws that I have put in my Word let people know the values and standards I call them to live by. To enter my presence and live in heaven they would need to keep the law exactly as required. That would be the only way they could come into my presence based on their own merit. The law is impossible for any person to keep. The standard is too high. Not only that. The person would only have to break the law in the smallest way to disqualify themself to be in my presence. My law will not bend to the will of people. My standard is 100% and anything less is abject failure. Getting close is not good enough. No human effort will get a person in a right standing with me through my law. People can only reach me by divine intervention. Every person has a list against their name of all the times they have broken my law. It is their debt of sin. But my Son has done for people what they could not earn or do for themselves. He was sinless. He fulfilled the law. He took each person's debt of sin and nailed it to the cross. He paid the debt for everyone and removed the barrier of the law. All through the Cross.

----o----

When you were dead in your sins and in the uncircumcision of your flesh, God made you alive with Christ. He forgave us all our sins, [14] having canceled the charge of our legal indebtedness, which stood against us and condemned us; he has taken it away, nailing it to the cross. [15] And having disarmed the powers and authorities, he made a public spectacle of them, triumphing over them by the cross. Colossians 2:13-15

----o----

4.

TWO FATHERHOODS

My Child . . .

As your Father you are a member of my family. You are my child because you have my Spirit within you. There are many who are not my children. Those who are not my children have Satan as their father. They may not understand that Satan is their father. But he is. When Adam sinned and turned away from me his Spiritual life connecting him to me died. One day he would also face physical death. I prohibited Adam and Eve from eating of the Tree of Knowledge of Good and Evil. I gave Adam the authority to rule over my creation. The tragedy is that Satan tricked Eve into eating of the Tree. Adam followed her lead without Satan tricking him. No longer would my Spirit be within them. The consequence was that Adam relinquished his rights to Satan. As a God who loves, I would need to one day restore the option of fellowship with my creation. Whilst at the same time dealing with the problem of Satan. The day would come. And all because of the Cross.

----o----

[42] Jesus said to them, "If God were your Father, you would love me, for I have come here from God. I have not come on my own; God sent me. [43] Why is my language not clear to you? Because you are unable to hear what I say. [44] You belong to your father, the devil, and you want to carry out your father's desires. He was a murderer from the beginning, not holding to the truth, for there is no truth in him. When he lies, he speaks his native language, for he is a liar and the father of lies. John 8:42-44

5.

SLAVERY TO SATAN

My Child . . .

The evil one, Satan, rules the current world system. This is the consequence of Adam's original sin. Your world lies in the power of the evil one. In effect everyone born is under slavery to him. This position of slavery did not apply to my Son because he was not born of a human father. His birthright was different. The evil one tried to bring my Son under his power. He tempted my Son with the offer of receiving all the kingdoms of the world if he would bow down to worship him. The temptation would not have been a temptation if the evil one did not have rights to the kingdoms. My Son did not dispute Satan's assertion. Had he taken up the offer it would have been sin. If he had sinned he would have come under slavery to the evil one. He would not have then been a free man who could pay the ransom price to set people free. That price was paid. And all because of the Cross.

⁸ Again, the devil took him to a very high mountain and showed him all the kingdoms of the world and their splendor. ⁹ "All this I will give you," he said, "if you will bow down and worship me." Matthew 4:8-9

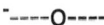

¹⁹ We know that we are children of God, and that the whole world is under the control of the evil one. 1 John 5:19

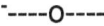

The god of this age has blinded the minds of unbelievers, so that they cannot see the light of the gospel that displays the glory of Christ, who is the image of God. 2 Corinthians 4:4

-----o----

6.

SPIRITUAL DEATH

My Child . . .

The consequence of sin is death. When Adam sinned he experienced death immediately. He experienced Spiritual death and separation from me. Physical death would come later. Once Adam sinned both Adam and Eve became alienated towards me. So much so that they tried to hide themselves from me. I had to find them guilty of sin and pronounce the death sentence on them. By implication, this sentence also fell on all their offspring. I had to banish them from the garden so they could not partake of the tree of life. Open access to me would no longer be available to them. Like a virus, Adam's sin has infected the whole human race. All people are born sinners and separated from me. Most will have to face physical death. Adam's sin led to absolute tragedy for my creation. In relation to me everyone is born Spiritually dead. Because of this they need reconciliation to me. They need to be Spiritually re-born to restore fellowship with me. My Son has made the way of restoration available to all people. And all because of the Cross.

----o----

[15] The Lord God took the man and put him in the Garden of Eden to work it and take care of it. [16] And the Lord God commanded the man, "You are free to eat from any tree in the garden; [17] but you must not eat from the tree of the knowledge of good and evil, for when you eat from it you will certainly die." Genesis 2:15-17

----o----

Therefore, just as sin entered the world through one man, and death through sin, and in this way death came to all people, because all sinned—Romans 5:12

----O----

Yet a time is coming and has now come when the true worshipers will worship the Father in the Spirit and in truth, for they are the kind of worshipers the Father seeks. ²⁴ God is spirit, and his worshipers must worship in the Spirit and in truth." John 4:23-24

----O----

7.

WALL OF SEPARATION

My Child . . .

Here is the full problem. The barriers that separate me from my creation are insurmountable for a person. Together they are like a wall that no one can scale. Only I could remove them. Everyone is born into sin and under the sentence of death. Spiritual life with me needs restoration. It is the only way to avoid the eternal consequences of separation from me. Adam surrendered his birthright to the evil one. Satan is the father of all unbelievers. The way to me is not by keeping the law. Keeping the law is impossible because no one can keep the law without failing at some point. It would be like trying to swim around the world. A person could get so far but nowhere near succeed. And I am holy. No one can approach me with their own holiness because no human can be holy and righteous of themselves. Here is my heart. My children are lost to me. I love them and want to be restored to them. I love them so much that I took the initiative to reach out to them. The barriers that separate me I have removed. I removed them in a way that showed my great love and desire for my creation. Reconciliation to me is now available. The cross was the only way to remove the barriers, offer restoration, and show my love. Only by the cross.

----o----

For God so loved the world that he gave his one and only Son, that whoever believes in him shall not perish but have eternal life. [17] For God did not send his Son into the world to condemn the world, but to save the world through him. [18] Whoever believes in him is not condemned, but whoever does not believe stands condemned already because they have not believed in the name of God's one and only Son. John 3:16-18

----o----

8.

COMMUNICATION

BREAKDOWN

My Child . . .

The barriers that separated me from my creation created a communication breakdown. I created Adam to communicate with me both in the natural realm and in the Spiritual realm. Holy Spirit was in him to enable communication with me at any time and in any place. The consequence of Spiritual death meant I could not communicate with Adam on a Spiritual level. I wanted to fix this problem. I wanted to be able to communicate my love to my creation. Imagine you see people cutting down trees in a forest. You can see the looming danger for all the creatures living in the forest. So you run to warn them of the impending danger and their possible death. But how do you tell them? How do you communicate with creatures who do not understand your words or actions. You love them so much and want to save their lives but you can't communicate the danger to them. The best way you could communicate to them would be to become one of them and speak to them on their terms. This is what I needed to do. So I sent my Son to become a part of the creation. God would no longer be distant from people. He would dwell among them and declare the way of salvation. And the Cross became the focal point of that declaration.

----o----

In the beginning was the Word, and the Word was with God, and the Word was God. ² He was with God in the beginning.   John 1:1-2

----o----

The Word became flesh and made his dwelling among us. We have seen his glory, the glory of the one and only Son, who came from the Father, full of grace and truth. John 1:14

----o----

9.

BEING FOUND

My Child . . .

Since the time of separation I have always wanted to be found by all peoples of the earth. I have often searched to find those whose heart is looking for me. Even when they do not realise themself that I am what they are looking for. I set in place times and lands in hope that hearts would recognise my hand and see my glory in what I have created. Sadly, many people choose to give glory to false gods who are no more than objects or ideas made by the hands and minds of people. In fact, having seen my creation they are without excuse. In all instances of my being found I have been the one to reach out to initiate the contact and relationship. People could be looking for answers but they only find them if I reach out and reveal things. I realise the enormity of the barriers that separate my creation from me. I recognise that no mere human can remove those barriers by their own will or strength. Sin has placed insurmountable obstacles between myself and all peoples. Insurmountable that is, by human effort. Only I could provide the requirements to make it possible for humanity to be reconciled to me. Only I could provide the solution to remove all barriers between myself and my creation. But, without my initiative and willingness to connect, no one would find me. I make it all work together for good. All through my Son and the Cross.

----o----

For the eyes of the Lord range throughout the earth to strengthen those whose hearts are fully committed to him. 2 Chronicles 16:9

----o----

²⁶ From one man he made all the nations, that they should inhabit the whole earth; and he marked out their appointed times in history and the boundaries of their lands. ²⁷ God did this so that they would seek him and perhaps reach out for him and find him, though he is not far from any one of us. Acts 17:26-27

----o----

For since the creation of the world God's invisible qualities—his eternal power and divine nature—have been clearly seen, being understood from what has been made, so that people are without excuse. Romans 1:20

----o----

10.

WAY TO FORGIVENESS

My Child . . .

For my creation to reconcile to me I needed to make a way to forgiveness possible. When Adam and Eve sinned they tried to hide their shame from me by wearing fig leaves they had sewn together. The fact that they felt they wanted to wear the fig leaves showed their new knowledge from disobeying me. I rejected their attempt to hide their sin by their own efforts. I rejected their clothing and provided animal skins to dress them with. In doing so I set a precedent. To provide the animal skins meant I had to kill an innocent victim. There had been no physical death of any creature up to this point. The animals had done nothing wrong to make them deserve death. This was to be my future pattern for people to receive forgiveness. The shed blood of an innocent substitute to provide forgiveness for a person. The shed blood, in effect, covers sin. This led to the Jewish system of sacrifice. An innocent animal offered and sacrificed according to my instructions. The blood of which covered an individuals and the nation's sin. It was only a temporary offering for sin. My plan was that one day a permanent offering would be sacrificed. Hence, my Son and the cross.

----o----

In fact, the law requires that nearly everything be cleansed with blood, and without the shedding of blood there is no forgiveness. Hebrews 9:22

----o----

How much more, then, will the blood of Christ, who through the eternal Spirit offered himself unblemished to God, cleanse our consciences from acts that lead to death, so that we may serve the living God! [15] For this reason Christ is the mediator of a new covenant, that those who are called may receive the promised eternal inheritance—now that he has died as a ransom to set them free from the sins committed under the first covenant. Hebrews 9:14-15

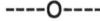

11.

PERFECT SACRIFICE

My Child . . .

Animal sacrifice for the forgiveness of sin was always going to be a temporary solution. Because sin came into the world because of a man, then the all-time solution to sin also needed to be through a man. What a man it would need to be. To qualify to being the perfect sacrifice I would need a perfect human substitute. He would need to be human and capable to live life and to die. He would need to be sinless. This means he would have to be born without a sin nature as Adam was. He would also need to live his life without sinning whilst at the same time open to temptation. He would need to live under the law and not break it at any point. He would need to understand

and accept the actions he was going to take. He would need to be willing to take upon himself people's guilt and judgement. To accept the guilty verdict others deserved and to die on their behalf. And the most difficult part of all. Forsaken by me. Forsaken by me so others would not have to suffer rejection. Only one person could qualify for such a task. Only one person could be the one and only sacrifice. My Son Jesus.

----o----

For just as through the disobedience of the one man the many were made sinners, so also through the obedience of the one man the many will be made righteous. Romans 5:19

----o----

For as in Adam all die, so in Christ all will be made alive. 1 Corinthians 15:22

----o----

12.

PROPHETIC GUIDANCE

My Child . . .

To enable people to know to look for the appearing of my Son, I gave prophets to prophesy of his coming. Through the prophets I let people know that the coming Messiah would be born of God. Born to a virgin. That he would be God in their midst. His names would include, Mighty God, Everlasting Father, Prince of Peace. I revealed that he would in fact be both God and man. God incarnate. He would be human and God. I made it known that he would be born in Bethlehem. I gave many details in many prophecies. I did not hide the amazing thing I was going to do. Even wise men from other nations came seeking him at his birth. My

Son would be perfect humanity and perfect deity for all to see. He indeed was the promised Messiah.

----o----

Therefore the Lord himself will give you a sign: The virgin will conceive and give birth to a son, and will call him Immanuel.(God with us)   Isaiah 7:14

----o----

For to us a child is born, to us a son is given, and the government will be on his shoulders. And he will be called Wonderful Counselor, Mighty God, Everlasting Father, Prince of Peace. Isaiah 9:6

----o----

"But you, Bethlehem Ephrathah, though you are small among the clans of Judah, out of you will come for me one who will be ruler over Israel, whose origins are from of old, from ancient times." Micah 5:2

13.

TWO ADAMS

My Child . . .

My Son is the second Adam. The first Adam brought death. The second Adam brought resurrection from the dead. He gave everlasting life to those who were Spiritually dead. He offers deliverance from sin and from the sentence of eternal separation from me. The first Adam, through disobedience, made everyone a sinner. But my second Adam, through obedience, makes many righteous. The first Adam brought condemnation through his act of rejecting my will. My Son makes it possible that there is no condemnation for those who belong to him. The first Adam got everyone born of man into distress. The second Adam came along to sort out the mess. Can you see the privileged position you are living in right now? You are now accepted by me in my Son. I love you with an everlasting love and will never disown you. You can now walk with me daily filled with the Holy Spirit, as my Son was. Jesus ever lives to make intercession for you. Many lived longing to experience what you have now but never tasted it. You receive it because of the cross.

----o----

For since death came through a man, the resurrection of the dead comes also through a man. ^{22} For as in Adam all die, so in Christ all will be made alive. I Corinthians 15:21-22

----o----

For if, by the trespass of the one man, death reigned through that one man, how much more will those who receive God's abundant provision of grace and of the gift of righteousness reign in life through the one man,

Jesus Christ! ¹⁸ Consequently, just as one trespass resulted in condemnation for all people, so also one righteous act resulted in justification and life for all people. ¹⁹ For just as through the disobedience of the one man the many were made sinners, so also through the obedience of the one man the many will be made righteous. Romans 5:17-19

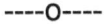

14.

JESUS THE MEDIATOR

My Child . . .

My Son became a mediator for all people. He is the one to mediate reconciliation between myself and humanity. In his humanity, as a mediator my Son understands the plight of mankind. He can mediate for them with compassion. He understands they cannot be reconciled to me by their own efforts. As God-the-Son he qualifies to approach me to make mediation. I can receive him because he is sinless and equal with me. In his humanity re represents mankind and in his deity he represents me. He is the only one qualified to equally represent both parties. No one else could undertake this task. My Son became a servant so that you and I could have fellowship. I wanted that from the moment I was separated from you. You can now approach me because the Mediator has reunited us. Because of Christ the Mediator you can call me Father, and I can call you my child. And if you fail at any time my Son ever lives to mediate for you.

----o----

"He is not a mere mortal like me that I might answer him, that we might confront each other in court.[33] If only there were someone to mediate between us, someone to bring us together,[34] someone to remove God's rod from me, so that his terror would frighten me no more.[35] Then I would speak up without fear of him, but as it now stands with me, I cannot. Job:932-35

----o----

[5] For there is one God and one mediator between God and mankind, the man Christ Jesus, 1 Timothy 2:5

15.

JESUS THE PRIEST

My Child . . .

As well as becoming the mediator between myself and all peoples, my Son also became a priest. As a priest my Son approaches me on behalf of others and represents their cause to me. As such, as a priest he is also an intercessor between people and myself. All other appointed priests carried out their duties while they were alive. However, their priesthood ceased when they died. My Son is different. He abides forever and therefore his priesthood abides forever. Because if this he is able to save those who come to me through him. And as he never dies he is always available to make intercession for you. He encompassed all requirements when he died once for all sin when he gave himself to the cross. My Son is perfect so he can do this on behalf of humanity. You have a great high priest who knew temptation in every area. He understands your weaknesses and has great love for you. Have confidence that when you approach me you will find mercy and compassion in your times of need. The cross has made sure of this.

----o----

[23] Now there have been many of those priests, since death prevented them from continuing in office; [24] but because Jesus lives forever, he has a permanent priesthood. [25] Therefore he is able to save completely those who come to God through him, because he always lives to intercede for them. [26] Such a high priest truly meets our need—one who is holy, blameless, pure, set apart from sinners, exalted above the heavens. [27] Unlike the other high priests, he does

not need to offer sacrifices day after day, first for his own sins, and then for the sins of the people. He sacrificed for their sins once for all when he offered himself. **28** For the law appoints as high priests men in all their weakness; but the oath, which came after the law, appointed the Son, who has been made perfect forever. Hebrews 7:23-28

----o----

Therefore, since we have a great high priest who has ascended into heaven,[f] Jesus the Son of God, let us hold firmly to the faith we profess. **15** For we do not have a high priest who is unable to empathize with our weaknesses, but we have one who has been tempted in every way, just as we are—yet he did not sin. **16** Let us then approach God's throne of grace with confidence, so that we may receive mercy and find grace to help us in our time of need. Hebrews 4:14-16

16.

JESUS THE REDEEMER

My Child . . .

Jesus came so that I could be revealed. By coming in human form Jesus showed by example what I was like. He showed people my character and love. He conveyed to the world that if they had seen him they have seen the me, the Father of all mankind. All that I wanted to reveal about myself to the world I revealed through my Son. He also revealed my plan of salvation. How I would make possible the redeeming of all peoples through the cross. Because his birth was as a direct descendent of King David, he qualifies to sit on the throne of David. Therefore, being born as a man, he could become the 'Kingsman Redeemer' to free people from slavery to the evil one. He still reveals me to you through the Holy Spirit. He is your reigning King of Kings. His redeeming power is available for you every day to overcome Satan. All because of the cross.

----o----

He will be great and will be called the Son of the Most High. The Lord God will give him the throne of his father David, [33] and he will reign over Jacob's descendants forever; his kingdom will never end." Luke 1:32-33

----o----

"……..I and the Father are one." John 10:30

----o----

In the past God spoke to our ancestors through the prophets at many times and in various ways, [2] but in these last days he has spoken to us by his Son, whom he appointed heir of all things, and through whom also he made the universe. ³ The Son is the radiance of God's glory and the exact representation of his being, sustaining all things by his powerful word. After he had provided purification for sins, he sat down at the right hand of the Majesty in heaven. Hebrews 1:1-3

17.

JESUS THE GOD MAN

My Child . . .

By what he said and how he lived Jesus showed that he was God in human form. No one else ever made all the claims about themselves as my Son did. He said that he came from God and that he was God. He received worship which was only reserved for God. He forgave people their sins which was something only God had the authority to do. He said he would raise from the dead, which he did. He said he would return to his Father's house to prepare a place for his followers. Which he did after they saw him ascend into heaven. Not only did my Son make claims but he also lived up to them. All his claims and the life he lived pointed to the fact that he was God incarnate. He qualified as the only person who could go to the cross to give his life. The only one who could make reconciliation with me a possibility for you. This not only showed my Son's great love for humanity. It also showed my Son's love for me. What a savior for the world! What a Son!

----o----

38 For I have come down from heaven not to do my will but to do the will of him who sent me. John 6:38

----o----

Then those who were in the boat worshiped him, saying, "Truly you are the Son of God." Matthew 14:33

----o----

But I want to know that the Son of Man has authority on earth to forgive sins." Matthew 9;6

----o----

18.

WHY THE CROSS?

My Child . . .

You may have wondered from time to time, why the cross? Why was the cross the only way for Jesus to reconcile people to me? The cross accomplishes many works. It removes the barriers between myself and mankind. The barriers are removed because of the long-standing history of sacrifice for sin. This was through my covenant with the nation of Israel. At the time Jesus arrived the nation of Israel practiced the Day of Atonement. This involved the shedding of the blood of an innocent victim on behalf of the nation's sins. On that day animals were sacrificed. Their blood was sprinkled on the Mercy Seat of the Arc of the Covenant by the High Priest. One sprinkling of blood was for the high priest's sins and the other for the sins of the nation. In my eyes, the shedding of the blood and it's sprinkling covered the individuals and nation's sin. When I saw the blood of an innocent victim I could forgive sins. This was a temporary measure. One day a once for all time sacrifice would be required. My Son became the once-for-all-time sacrifice. Without the shedding of blood there is no forgiveness for sin. Which is why you can receive forgiveness today because of what my Son achieved so long ago. Why the cross? Because it openly needed to be seen that I was prepared to allow my Son to take on himself the sins of the whole world. It was a witness to all humanity and to the powers in spiritual realms. Victory over sin and death was secured. Once for all. By the way of the cross.

----o----

It is impossible for the blood of bulls and goats to take away sins. Hebrews 10:4

----o----

11 Day after day every priest stands and performs his religious duties; again and again he offers the same sacrifices, which can never take away sins. 12 But when this priest had offered for all time one sacrifice for sins, he sat down at the right hand of God, 13 and since that time he waits for his enemies to be made his footstool. 14 For by one sacrifice he has made perfect forever those who are being made holy. Hebrews 10 11-14

----o----

19.

WRATH OF GOD

My Child . . .

I can be a God of wrath. I know this seems to go against my being a God of love. I understand how that can seem difficult for you. Always remember that I am a God of justice. Justice must be served for an offence. There has been a violation, sin, and it must be dealt with. I cannot compromise. If I compromised then the work of the cross would be to no avail. Everyone has the choice to believe my Son has suffered my wrath on their behalf. My Son has taken my wrath for all. If rejected they will face my wrath against them at a future time of judgment. My desire is that all people would accept the work of Jesus at the cross in taking my wrath for them. Whoever does that then open themselves up to receiving my love on intimate levels. Such a great price paid to make this possible. My Son becoming forsaken by me and receiving punishment for sin he had never committed. My wrath is no longer a threat to you for your past, present, or future sins. My wrath taken out on my Son. My Son loved you so much! Such is the work of the cross.

----o----

Whoever believes in the Son has eternal life, but whoever rejects the Son will not see life, for God's wrath remains on them. John 3:36

----o----

20.

WRATH REMOVED

My Child . . .

My Son did not only turn away my wrath for those who believe in him now. He also turned away my wrath for those who lived by faith in the Old Testament who lived before the cross. The removal of my wrath is possible because of the following. It means that where there has been an offence that is worthy of wrath. that wrath can be turned away after justice has been satisfied. It also allows for what was once alienated to be reconciled. This act of the cross means that people can be reconciled to me. The deserved wrath is turned away. But it goes further. Not only can people be free from my deserved wrath. Their reconciliation to me means they can live afresh under my covenant of grace. Coming to me by faith based on the 'take God's wrath in my place' sacrifice of my Son allows this. Justice is legally satisfied.

----o----

God presented Christ as a sacrifice of atonement, through the shedding of his blood—to be received by faith. He did this to demonstrate his righteousness, because in his forbearance he had left the sins committed beforehand unpunished— [26] he did it to demonstrate his righteousness at the present time, so as to be just and the one who justifies those who have faith in Jesus. Romans 3:25-26

----o----

21.

CERTIFICATE OF DEBT

My Child . . .

Sin imprisons people. Innocence was broken and sin entered in. A debt needed paying. The debt of sin. Each time a person sins the list of sins on the debt grows longer and longer. Each sin reveals that the judgement for sin is correct. When a Roman citizen was convicted of a crime they incurred a Certificate of Debt. This was an actual certificate that listed the crimes and the penalty that was due to be paid. If the citizen was put in jail the Certificate of Debt was nailed to the cell door. This meant that everyone could see the person's crimes listed against them. They could see the appropriate punishment and lawful imprisonment. The certificate remained on the door until their time was up and thus having paid for their crimes. In my eyes each person has their own Certificate of Debt. A list of sins that reveals a debt has to be paid. The wages of sin is death. My judgement of Spiritual and physical death is correct and payable. Imprisoned by sin the person cannot pay the price to escape their jail cell. But my Son has paid the price on the cross. The sentence that is due and freedom from the debt of sin is now available to those who want it. My Son took the guilt upon himself for every listed sin for every person's debt of sin and nailed it to the cross. Your debt of sin is paid in full! And it is paid for all time.

----o----

When you were dead in your sins and in the uncircumcision of your flesh, God made you alive with Christ. He forgave us all our sins, [14] having canceled the charge of our legal indebtedness, which stood against us and condemned us; he has taken it away, nailing it to the cross. Colossians 2:13-14

22.

FORSAKEN

My Child . . .

Jesus was forsaken by me so that you would not have to be. My Son cried out from the cross, "My God My God, why have You forsaken me?" I brought darkness over the earth. My wrath against sin was taken out on my Son. He took the punishment for every sin of every person upon himself and became forsaken by me. My wrath was poured out on him. For the first and only time my Son was separated from Holy Spirit and me. Totally God forsaken for the sins of the world. This was the greatest cost. There has never been a loneliness like it. And all voluntarily for me and for you to be able to be reconciled to one another. Never forget this abundant cost. Salvation is a free gift but was purchased at the highest cost possible. My Son, separated from every person he had ever loved. Hanging on that cross alone. Truly and totally alone. So that you and I would never have to be alone.

----o----

My God, my God, why have you forsaken me? Why are you so far from saving me, so far from my cries of anguish? Psalm 22:1

----o----

And at three in the afternoon Jesus cried out in a loud voice, *"Eloi, Eloi, lema sabachthani?"* (which means "My God, my God, why have you forsaken me?"). Mark 15:34

----o----

23.

IT IS FINISHED

My Child . . .

"My God My God, why have You forsaken me?" brought the creation to one of its most darkest moments. The cry of "It is finished," resounded around the world as a call of victory. At that moment the victory of the cross was secured for all time. All that would follow in the ministry of my Son was grounded in that victory. It was at this point that the Certificate of Debt was paid in full. It also signalled the victory over death as on the third day the glorious resurrection of my Son took place. But two other significant victories were won that day. Victory from slavery to Satan. Victory over the flesh, the internal sin nature of the whole of humanity. A complete victory was achieved by my Son that made redemption available for all people. A full redemption for those who would put faith in my Son and his work on the cross on their behalf. Faith to believe in being set free instead of remaining imprisoned in their sin. My Son is the only way of redemption. He has paid the highest price to redeem those under slavery to the world, the flesh, and the Devil. What was impossible for a person, made possible by me. All achieved by my Son and the cross. Hold on to these truths.

When he had received the drink, Jesus said, "It is finished." With that, he bowed his head and gave up his spirit. John 19:30

Keep watch over yourselves and all the flock of which the Holy Spirit has made you overseers. Be shepherds of the church of God, which he bought with his own blood. ²⁹ I know that after I leave, savage wolves will come in among you and will not spare the flock. ³⁰ Even from your own number men will arise and distort the truth in order to draw away disciples after them. ³¹ So be on your guard! Acts 20:28-31a

24.

FREEDOM FROM SLAVERY

My Child . . .

Redemption has brought freedom to you. You are set free in my Son. Do not consider your freedom as a license to live anyway you want to. When you consider the freedom my Son has won for you, think not of only freedom itself. Think on the price paid for your freedom. Think of a slave market. Before you were 'born again' in my Son, you were a member of the slave market. Enslaved by sin, the world, and the Devil. You were on public display in the slave market place and at the mercy of your captors. Your slave masters only brought deepening slavery and no hope of freedom. The only hope you had was if someone could pay the price to buy your freedom from the slave masters.

Someone who could redeem you. The cost of your freedom is the blood of my Son. It's was the only thing that could seal the deal. You have become a member of my family by the work of the cross. You are to no longer live for yourself but for Him who paid for your freedom. This is your reasonable response.

----o----

We know that we are children of God, and that the whole world is under the control of the evil one. 1 John 5:19

----o----

Christ redeemed us from the curse of the law by becoming a curse for us, for it is written: "Cursed is everyone who is hung on a pole." Galatians 3:13

----o----

For you know that it was not with perishable things such as silver or gold that you were redeemed from the empty way of life handed down to you from your ancestors, [19] but with the precious blood of Christ, a lamb without blemish or defect. 1 Peter:18-19

25.

QUALIFIED REDEEMER

My Child . . .

Not anyone could become your redeemer. I could only allow a redeemer who met the correct guidelines. It needed to be someone who was without sin. My Son qualified. It would need to be someone who was not under slavery to the evil one. Because my Son had never sinned and because he was not born of Adam's seed, he had no inherited sin. He did not come under Satan's control. My Son thereby qualified again. The redeemer needed to be human so that blood could be shed. Without the shedding of blood there in no forgiveness for sin. Again, my Son qualified. The redeemer also needed to be able to mediate between humanity and myself. Because of his humanity, my Son can approach me on behalf of others. Because of His deity he can approach me based on his divinity. He is the perfect mediator between me and humanity. The redeemer also needed to be willing to lay down their own life. By their own free will offer their life as a sacrifice for sin. My Son did this. Only my Son could be your redeemer. No one else could qualify. What a blessing my Son is for me and for you.

----o----

but with the precious blood of Christ, a lamb without blemish or defect. 1 Peter 1:19

----o----

Now a slave has no permanent place in the family, but a son belongs to it forever. John 8:35

----o----

Since the children have flesh and blood, he too shared in their humanity so that by his death he might break the power of him who holds the power of death—that is, the devil— Hebrews 2:14-15

----o----

For there is one God and one mediator between God and mankind, the man Christ Jesus, [6] who gave himself as a ransom for all people. 1 Tim 2:5-6a

----o----

The reason my Father loves me is that I lay down my life—only to take it up again. [18] No one takes it from me, but I lay it down of my own accord. I have authority to lay it down and authority to take it up again. This command I received from my Father." John 10:17-18

----o----

26.

JESUS THE GIFT?

My Child . . .

My Son is my Gift to the world. He has paid the cost of redemption for everyone. There is no cost for anyone to pay to enter into my salvation. But there is a choice. All are welcome but only a few will choose to accept my gift. My gift of redemption is like any other gift. If a person hands a gift out to you, you have a choice. Do you reach out and accept the gift or do you reject taking the gift? It is the same for people with my Son. Do they want to accept my Son's gift of salvation or not? I will not force anyone to receive my gift. I have to allow people to use their own free will. They have to come in faith. If they will confess with their mouth that, "Jesus is Lord," and believe in their heart that he raised from the dead, then they will be saved. By my power they will become my child, as you are. That is the bottom line. No strings attached. It is a gift too good to refuse. But people do. Anyone who spends eternity separated from me will ultimately do so because they chose to.

----o----

"Come to me, all you who are weary and burdened, and I will give you rest. ^{29} Take my yoke upon you and learn from me, for I am gentle and humble in heart, and you will find rest for your souls. ^{30} For my yoke is easy and my burden is light." Matthew 11:28-30

----o----

If you declare with your mouth, "Jesus is Lord," and believe in your heart that God raised him from the dead, you will be saved. Romans 10:9

----o----

Yet to all who did receive him, to those who believed in his name, he gave the right to become children of God— ¹³ children born not of natural descent, nor of human decision or a husband's will, but born of God.

John 1:12-13

27.

SUBSTITUTIONARY DEATH

My Child . . .

You know my Son died for you. I want you to understand that he not only died for you but he died in your place. It was you who deserved to die. That is the penalty and judgement for sin. My Son had no sin, but he took the punishment for your sin. That was his substitutionary death on your behalf. Adam and Eve experienced spiritual death followed by physical death. What a shock it was for them to see their deceased son. You often hear of or see death. My Son's substitutionary death was not only for this life. There is a second death. This will be an eternal death. This will be the everlasting state of a person. It will not be a death with no memory or feelings. The second death will be a state on consciousness for eternity. Those who reject my Son will be in a state of remorse for the whole of their never-ending existence. And separated from me. You are my child. You have believed in and accepted the finished work of my Son on the Cross. You accept his death in your place. The second death will not have any power over you. Eternal life with me has already begun for you.

----o----

"He answered, 'Then I beg you, father, send Lazarus to my family, [28] for I have five brothers. Let him warn them, so that they will not also come to this place of torment.' [29] "Abraham replied, 'They have Moses and the Prophets; let them listen to them.'

[30] "'No, father Abraham,' he said, 'but if someone from the dead goes to them, they will repent.' [31] "He said to him, 'If they do not listen to Moses and the Prophets,

they will not be convinced even if someone rises from the dead.'" Luke 16:27-31

----o----

Then I saw a great white throne and him who was seated on it. The earth and the heavens fled from his presence, and there was no place for them. [12] And I saw the dead, great and small, standing before the throne, and books were opened. Another book was opened, which is the book of life. The dead were judged according to what they had done as recorded in the books. [13] The sea gave up the dead that were in it, and death and Hades gave up the dead that were in them, and each person was judged according to what they had done. [14] Then death and Hades were thrown into the lake of fire. The lake of fire is the second death. [15] Anyone whose name was not found written in the book of life was thrown into the lake of fire. Revelation 20:11-15

28.

ONE LAMB FOR FEW

My Child . . .

When it came time for me to release my people from slavery to Egypt I established The Passover. I told Moses to tell Pharaoh that if he still refused to let my people go and remove their slavery I would bring a night of judgement over the land of Egypt. Every firstborn of all animals and families would perish. This included Egyptian and Hebrew families. I allowed my own people to be subject to the coming judgement. But I gave them a way of escape. To deliver my people I provided that they could kill a lamb and sprinkle its blood over the door and doorposts. When the angel of death moved over the land, wherever it saw the blood it would 'pass over' that house. The judgment of death was not carried out on the inhabitants of those houses. Those households gained my salvation. Any household without the protection of the blood would face the judgement of the death of its firstborn. This was such an important occasion for Israel to remember. I established that The Passover be celebrated every year as a reminder of my salvation. It highlighted the importance of sacrificial blood and it was the forerunner of what was to come. This was only sacrificial blood for one household. Better was to come.

----o----

Tell the whole community of Israel that on the tenth day of this month each man is to take a lamb for his family, one for each household. ⁴ If any household is too small for a whole lamb, they must share one with their nearest neighbor, having taken into account the number of people there are. You are to determine the amount of lamb needed in accordance with what each person will eat. ⁵ The animals you choose must be year-old males without defect, and you may take them from the sheep or the goats. ⁶ Take care of them until the fourteenth day of the month, when all the members of the community of Israel must slaughter them at twilight. ⁷ Then they are to take some of the blood and put it on the sides and tops of the doorframes of the houses where they eat the lambs. Exodus 12:3-7

"On that same night I will pass through Egypt and strike down every firstborn of both people and animals, and I will bring judgment on all the gods of Egypt. I am the Lord. ¹³ The blood will be a sign for you on the houses where you are, and when I see the blood, I will pass over you. No destructive plague will touch you when I strike Egypt.¹⁴ "This is a day you are to commemorate; for the generations to come you shall celebrate it as a festival to the Lord—a lasting ordinance. Exodus 12:12-14

29.

TWO GOATS ALL ISRAEL

My Child . . .

I instructed Moses to make a building that would be transportable. It was for worship and sacrifice. It was the 'Tabernacle.' It consisted of an outdoor area where animal sacrifices could take place, and two rooms on the inside. One room was the 'Holy Place' and contained items for worshipping me. The second room was the 'Holy of Holies,' and was the room where the Ark of the Covenant was. It was also the place where my presence dwelt above the Ark. The Ark had a gold lid which is called the Mercy Seat. I ordained that each year a High Priest was to select two goats, sacrifice one and take the blood and sprinkle it on the mercy seat. When I saw the blood of the innocent victim it would satisfy my wrath for the sins of the nation for a year. The other goat was released into the wilderness as a symbol that the nation's sins had been take away. This day became known as the 'Day of Atonement'. In Egypt the lamb was for one night. In the Tabernacle the goats were for one nation for a whole year. Neither of these were my perfect option. That was still to come.

----o----

The law is only a shadow of the good things that are coming—not the realities themselves. For this reason it can never, by the same sacrifices repeated endlessly year after year, make perfect those who draw near to worship. [2] Otherwise, would they not have stopped being offered? For the worshipers would have been cleansed once for all, and would no longer have felt guilty for their sins. [3] But those sacrifices are an annual reminder of sins. [4] It is impossible for the blood of bulls and goats to take away sins. Hebrews 10:1-4

30.

THE ULTIMATE LAMB

My Child . . .

An innocent animal's blood shed so that Adam and Eve could be clothed. A lamb sacrificed so that each Hebrew household could be saved from the death of its firstborn. A lamb sacrificed for the nation of Israel to pay for their sins for a year. It was not my plan that any of these would be permanent. And they were not. At the right time the true Lamb appeared. My Son. It was no mistake that my Son was called the 'Lamb of God.' He is the final and once-for-all sacrifice for sin. Not just for some individuals. Not just for one household. Not even for just one nation. He is the 'Lamb of God' for the whole world. My Son became the permanent solution for the problem of sin. He is the only way a person's sin can be forgiven by me. There is no other name by which people can gain salvation from sin and death. He is the only way to me. Why do you think His crucifixion took place on the day of Passover? He was the true Passover Lamb. My judgement passes-over you because I see your faith in His shed blood.

----o----

The next day John saw Jesus coming toward him and said, "Look, the Lamb of God, who takes away the sin of the world! John 1:29.

----o----

But we do see Jesus, who was made lower than the angels for a little while, now crowned with glory and honor because he suffered death, so that by the grace of God he might taste death for everyone. Hebrews 2:9

----o----

God made him who had no sin to be sin for us, so that in him we might become the righteousness of God. 2 Corinthians 5:21

31.

RECONCILIATION

My Child . . .

Reconciliation is a special word to me. In the natural world it means that two people who were at enmity can be restored to a new relationship. It is a special word to me because of what my Son has achieved by the cross. I can restore a person into fellowship with me because of three things accomplished by the cross. My wrath has been satisfied. Redemption is possible because the slavery ransom was paid. The sentence of death has been served by the death of my Son. Because of these my relationship with my creation can be established again. It can be reconciled. I've always wanted to be reconciled. My heart has never changed in regards to wanting fellowship with people. But it was not possible until my Son became the way and the truth and the life. Until he broke down the barriers preventing reconciliation to me. Legal reconciliation can now take place. It is great joy to me that you have personally been reconciled to me. That you have trusted in the work of my Son and been brought into fellowship with me. Tell others reconciliation is possible for them.

----o----

Jesus answered, "I am the way and the truth and the life. No one comes to the Father except through me. John 14:6

----o----

Therefore, if anyone is in Christ, the new creation has come: The old has gone, the new is here! [18] All this is from God, who reconciled us to himself through Christ and gave us the ministry of reconciliation: [19] that

God was reconciling the world to himself in Christ, not counting people's sins against them. And he has committed to us the message of reconciliation. [20] We are therefore Christ's ambassadors, as though God were making his appeal through us. We implore you on Christ's behalf: Be reconciled to God. [21] God made him who had no sin to be sin for us, so that in him we might become the righteousness of God. 2 Corinthians 5:17-21

32.

NO HOSTILITY

My Child . . .

    I hold no hostility toward you or any of my children. You do not need to be defensive towards me. I am not looking at your life and counting each sin and building hostility against you once again. My Son took the hostility on your behalf. My anger towards you because of your sins was all dealt with at the cross. It is good for you to realize and have peace in your mind that the matter is dealt with. Your sin is forgiven and you are reconciled to me. Don't build up hostility and alienation towards me in your minds. I love you and want you to experience my love to the fullest. Always rely on the work of my Son on the Cross and not on your own works. Keep the cross central in your walk with me. The victory of the cross is a constant foundation for your Christian life. That victory never changes. What it has achieved never ceases to be what you need to live for my Son and I with guidance from Holy Spirit.

----o----

For God was pleased to have all his fullness dwell in him, [20] and through him to reconcile to himself all things, whether things on earth or things in heaven, by making peace through his blood, shed on the cross. [21] Once you were alienated from God and were enemies in your minds because of your evil behavior. [22] But now he has reconciled you by Christ's physical body through death to present you holy in his sight, without blemish and free from accusation— Colossians 1:19-22

----o----

33.

JUSTIFICATION

My Child . . .

I have always been a God of mercy. If I was not merciful I would not have found a way for you to be reconciled to me. But I did. I found a way so that my holy wrath could be satisfied so that I could act with grace towards you. I have justified you in my sight. I look for those with a humble heart. By a humble heart I mean a heart that understands where is stands before me. A person with a humble heart knows that there is nothing they can do to make themselves acceptable to me. Their heart knows they need me to make the move to accept them. This is why I have justified you. The forgiveness of your sins was required. But more was required. Your sins needed to be dealt with effectively, which was achieved by my Son. But you needed something else added to you in order to be fully justified. That too was given to you by the work of my Son. Not only are your sins forgiven, but you have been given the righteousness of Christ. He took your sins and gave you his righteousness. You were justified and declared righteous the moment you believed and put your faith in my Son.

----o----

To some who were confident of their own righteousness and looked down on everyone else, Jesus told this parable: **10** "Two men went up to the temple to pray, one a Pharisee and the other a tax collector. **11** The Pharisee stood by himself and prayed: 'God, I thank you that I am not like other people—robbers, evildoers, adulterers—or even like this tax collector. **12** I fast twice a week and give a tenth of all I get.'¹³ "But the tax collector stood at a distance. He would not even look up to heaven, but beat his breast and said, 'God, have mercy on me, a sinner.' ¹⁴ "I tell you that this man, rather than the other, went home justified before God. For all those who exalt themselves will be humbled, and those who humble themselves will be exalted." Luke 18:9-14

34.

BY FAITH

My Child . . .

Throughout church history there have been tensions about being declared righteous and living a righteous life. I want you to understand fully that you are to live by faith. You are not to develop a righteousness of your own by your own human merits. Do not endeavour to do works that are works that are exclusively done by me. I have bestowed the righteousness of my Son on you. This is permanent. I know there is a tension for you in your daily life. I say you are righteous and yet you fail to live the righteousness my word calls you to live. This is why you must call on Holy Spirt to live the Christian life through you. It's why you still need my Son to intercede for you. I know you will fail to live to the standards I set. When you sin, confess and receive forgiveness. When you don't know how to live ask Holy Spirit to teach you and guide you. It is a fine line for you to walk. I have allowed that on purpose. I have allowed it so you will need to call on me and all my resources to learn how to walk by faith. I do this because I want you to draw close to me and allow me to be a Father to you.

----o----

For in the gospel the righteousness of God is revealed—a righteousness that is by faith from first to last, just as it is written: "The righteous will live by faith." Romans 1:17

----o----

35.

NO CONFIDENCE

My Child . . .

The question of righteousness in your life is an important one. I do not want my children to put any confidence in their flesh. This means I do not want you to trust in any way that by keeping the law you are living a righteous life the way I want you to. For example, the circumcised person that I call to worship me is one who is circumcised in their heart. And who worships me in the Spirit and puts no confidence in the deeds or rituals of their flesh. It's not about looking into my law and working to fulfill it 100 percent. Your flesh can never achieve such a lofty goal. You may think 70 percent is good enough. Maybe 90 percent is just about perfect. The problem is, my acceptance level for you is 100 percent righteousness. That is why I have provided that for you through my Son. You cannot achieve it any other way. Do not be deceived by 'do-gooders' who say you must carry out acts to make yourself righteous. Be on your guard that no one lays a 'guilt trip' on you to put your trust in your flesh. My Son has dealt with that for you.

----o----

For it is we who are the circumcision, we who serve God by his Spirit, who boast in Christ Jesus, and who put no confidence in the flesh— [4] though I myself have reasons for such confidence. If someone else thinks they have reasons to put confidence in the flesh, I have more: [5] circumcised on the eighth day, of the people of Israel, of the tribe of Benjamin, a Hebrew of Hebrews; in regard to the law, a Pharisee; [6] as for zeal, persecuting the church; as for righteousness based on the law, faultless.⁷ But whatever were gains to me I now consider loss for the sake of Christ. ⁸ What is more, I consider everything a loss because of the surpassing worth of knowing Christ Jesus my Lord, for whose sake I have lost all things. I consider them garbage, that I may gain Christ ⁹ and be found in him, not having a righteousness of my own that comes from the law, but that which is through faith in Christ—the righteousness that comes from God on the basis of faith. Philippians 3:2-9

----o----

36.

PEACE

My Child . . .

See yourself as I see you. Don't view yourself on how you feel at any particular moment in time. Don't think of yourself as having to live by super high standards in order to meet my approval. You have peace with me. It's because you are justified in my sight that you have peace with me. Don't live as if your relationship with me is fragile and can easily be broken. Always remember that the cross deals with your past, present, and future. The cross has won peace for you for all of your days. Your past is dealt with and we have peace. Your daily life now is one of walking in peace with me. Your future is one of eternal peace, again due to the cross. Make sure you are believing by faith in the righteousness of my Son which makes you at peace with me. Don't live in fear of my rejecting you when you fail to live as you know you should. You are now standing in my grace and I will always seek the best for you no matter what may happen between us. Accept my peace, through my Son, by faith.

----o----

Therefore, since we have been justified through faith, we have peace with God through our Lord Jesus Christ, [2] through whom we have gained access by faith into this grace in which we now stand. And we boast in the hope of the glory of God. Romans 5:1-2

----o----

37.

NO CONDEMNATION

My Child . . .

Because you are justified in my sight you are not condemned by me anymore. If you are living under what you perceive as condemnation, rest assured it is not from me. Many live under self-condemnation and imagine it's from me. You will never be under my condemnation now that you are 'born again' in my Son. If others condemn you for not living as they think you should, do not take their condemnation upon yourself. You don't need to feel guilty for what others think about you. Remember what I think about you. You are not condemned because of my Son's redemptive work on the cross. My Son was your substitute to take my condemnation for you. The matter is now settled. You have passed from death to life in my Son. I cannot undo that work. It is finished! Your behaviour does not bring you under my condemnation. Relax. The matter is sorted. You can live for me without any condemnation and in dependence on the indwelling Holy Spirit. When you fail there is intercession, confession, forgiveness and renewal. But no condemnation.

----o----

"Very truly I tell you, whoever hears my word and believes him who sent me has eternal life and will not be judged but has crossed over from death to life. John 5:24

----o----

Therefore, there is now no condemnation for those who are in Christ Jesus, [2] because through Christ Jesus the law of the Spirit who gives life has set you free from the law of sin and death. Romans 8:1-2

38.

ME FOR YOU

My Child . . .

Always remember that I am for you and as such who can really be against you? When I defend you, who is going to overcome me against you? No one is powerful enough to overcome me. I gave up my most precious Son for you. If I can freely give my Son for you, how could I not freely provide all you need now? If I did so much for you when you were my enemy, imagine the abundance I can do for you now you are my reconciled child! Where are your accusers now that I accept you fully? No one is qualified to be your accuser because I accept you as righteous. My Son will not accuse you because I have declared you righteous with his righteousness. You see, I love you with an everlasting love. My love for you will not allow you to be separated from my love for you. My Son and I never will allow you to be separated from our love. There is nothing in the whole of creation that can cause that to happen.

----o----

What, then, shall we say in response to these things? If God is for us, who can be against us? [32] He who did not spare his own Son, but gave him up for us all—how will he not also, along with him, graciously give us all things? [33] Who will bring any charge against those whom God has chosen? It is God who justifies.

[37] No, in all these things we are more than conquerors through him who loved us. [38] For I am convinced that neither death nor life, neither angels nor demons, neither the present nor the future, nor any powers, [39] neither height nor depth, nor anything else

in all creation, will be able to separate us from the love of God that is in Christ Jesus our Lord. Romans 8:31-33, 37-39

39.

THE ACCUSER

My Child . . .

There will be one who will accuse you. The evil one. The Devil. Your adversary, Satan. He will accuse you and try and make you believe it is me accusing you. So be well aware that I will never accuse you. He will take great joy if he can make you accuse yourself. This is why you need to stand in faith on what my Son has achieved for you at the cross. Stand in that victory. Accusations and any condemnation do not come from me. Don't believe the words of your enemy but believe my words. Focus on my Son and what he has done for you. Rest in the truth that you are declared righteous on the basis of faith and nothing else. It has been graciously given to you as a gift of salvation. Be assured it's not about you but all about my Son. Rest in his works.

----o----

Be alert and of sober mind. Your enemy the devil prowls around like a roaring lion looking for someone to devour. 1Peter 5:8

----o----

"Now have come the salvation and the power and the kingdom of our God, and the authority of his Messiah. For the accuser of our brothers and sisters, who accuses them before our God day and night, has been hurled down. [11] They triumphed over him by the blood of the Lamb and by the word of their testimony; they did not love their lives so much as to shrink from death. Revelation 12:10

----o----

40.

TOTAL FORGIVENESS

My Child . . .

I have forgiven you with a total forgiveness. I have forgiven your past, present, and future sins. Not only have I forgiven them. I have forgot all about them. This is not because I now make light of your sin. Sin in your life had to be dealt with fully. It would be of no use to forgive you and accept you and then see you sin again and reject you. At the cross my son has given you a full redemption. You were dead in your sins. That is the state of everyone before turning to my Son. I have made you alive in my Son. All your sins are forgiven. When I say this I am referring to a time in the past. When I dealt with them. This was at the cross. Because of that one act I forgive your sin for all time.

'All' means every sin and excludes no sin. Be clear on this. I am not just meaning the sins before you knew my Son. How many of your sins were in the future when my Son died on the cross? All of them! Rejoice! The cross is a complete work for your sin!

----o----

Then he adds: "Their sins and lawless acts I will remember no more." Hebrews 10:17

----o----

When you were dead in your sins and in the uncircumcision of your flesh, God made you alive with Christ. He forgave us all our sins, Colossians 2:13

----o----

41.

FORGIVENESS TOO

My Child . . .

I have forgiven your sins and now you can live with the fruit of forgiveness. If I can forgive you then you have the ability to forgive yourself. There may be past sins you have committed that you are still feeling guilty about. What good will feeling guilty about your past sins do for you? I have forgiven them all. Take time now to forgive yourself for those sins you still think about. Remember that I have forgiven and forgotten your sins. Forgive yourself and forget about those sins forever. I am not holding things against you for your sins so don't hold things against yourself. Don't think I don't understand how bad your sins have been. I gave my son on the cross because of your sins. What more could I do? As well as forgiving yourself you can now forgive others. You're forgiven, now go and forgive others. I forgave your wrongs towards me. Now forgive those wrongs others have committed against you. Are your standards higher than mine? The sin that you cannot forgive is one that my Son died for. I forgive you. Forgive yourself and others.

----o----

I am writing to you, dear children, because your sins have been forgiven on account of his name. 1 John 2:12

----o----

Bear with each other and forgive one another if any of you has a grievance against someone. Forgive as the Lord forgave you. Colossians 3:13

----o----

42.

FOCUS

My Child . . .

There is now no reason for you to focus on sin in your life. The work of my Son on the cross is a complete work. When you sin, instead of focusing on the sin focus on what you can immediately do about it. Confess your sin and ask forgiveness. If you recognise sin and do not confess it then Holy Spirt will keep reminding you of the sin so you can deal with it. If you keep ignoring Holy Spirit then in my love I may have to discipline you for your own benefit. My discipline is not a punishment for your sin. My discipline is my way or reminding you and teaching you to deal with the obvious sin in your life. You don't have to worry about punishment for sin from me. My Son took the punishment. Confess it, receive forgiveness and move on. Forgiveness is always available no matter how many times you sin. My focus is not on your sin but on teaching you how to walk in the Holy Spirit. I want you to focus on walking in the Spirit.

----o----

. . . ,but God disciplines us for our good, in order that we may share in his holiness. Hebrews 12:10b

----o----

So I say, walk by the Spirit, and you will not gratify the desires of the flesh. Galatians 5:16

----o----

43.

BAPTISM INTO DEATH

My Child . . .

Death has no power over my Son. Because of his death and resurrection he cannot die again. The wonderful truth of that for you is that you have died with him through baptism. In effect you are raised from the dead in him to walk in newness of life. Death has no hold on you now. Yes, you may face physical death in this life, but you now have eternal life. Once you leave this life you will continue to live forever in the fulfillment of the new life my Son won for you. So believe that you have died with my Son. Believe also that you will live with him. This is why sin no longer has a right to control your life. My Son died for your sin and you died in him. So now you can live as being dead to sin. Do not live under submission to sin. Fight it with the fact that you are dead to it. Oh yes, it will try hard, very hard, to control your life. Don't let it. Offer your life as a living sacrifice to me. Every part of you.

----o----

What shall we say, then? Shall we go on sinning so that grace may increase? ² By no means! We are those who have died to sin; how can we live in it any longer? ³ Or don't you know that all of us who were baptized into Christ Jesus were baptized into his death? ⁴ We were therefore buried with him through baptism into death in order that, just as Christ was raised from the dead through the glory of the Father, we too may live a new life. Romans 6:1-4

----o----

44.

PENALTY AND POWER

My Child . . .

Your freedom in my Son has two very important aspects for your daily life. You have freedom from the penalty of sin by the death of my Son for you. That removed the barrier between us. The second important aspect is that I have provided for you a daily deliverance from the power of sin. My Son died to sin. So, not only did he die for sin, but he also lived for me. This is why you should consider yourself dead to sin and alive to me through my Son. Legally, sin has been dealt with. Its penalty is dealt with. But it's power and control over your life is up to you. As my child you need to claim the victory over sin. Not just that. Claim the victory and depend on the indwelling Holy Spirit to overcome sins attacks. Sin is now like an illegal immigrant trying to invade your life. It has no legal right to be there but it still seeks to make a home for itself. It is relentless. When sin tempts you, rest assured I will give you a way of escape. As you trust in the Holy Spirit your conflict with sin will turn out to strengthen your faith.

----o----

For what I received I passed on to you as of first importance: that Christ died for our sins according to the Scriptures, 1 Corinthians 15:3

----o----

The death he died, he died to sin once for all; but the life he lives, he lives to God. Romans 6:10

----o----

No temptation has overtaken you except what is common to mankind. And God is faithful; he will not let you be tempted beyond what you can bear. But when you are tempted, he will also provide a way out so that you can endure it. 1 Corinthians 10:13

45.

THE LAW AND SATAN

My Child . . .

Satan will try to use the Law against you. The Law helps you to recognise what is and isn't sin. You cannot live by the standards of the Law. That is to say that trying to keep the Law in your own strength will always fail. When you see the Law and think you should be living better it's time to beware. The danger being that you think you are failing me and that you are unworthy in my site. Keeping the Law to the best of your ability can never make you worthy in my sight. You are worthy because you have put faith in what my Son has done for you. That is the only way to being worthy in my sight. Satan will try and use the Law against you. He will tell you that you are not living as I would want you to. He will point out all your failings and get you to look to the Law to put things right in your life. He wants to get your eyes off my Son and Holy Spirit. He wants to try and trick you into living in your own strength and abilities and not to trust in mine. Remember that without my Son and the Holy Spirit you can do nothing to live the Christian life. When you think you should be doing better ask the Holy Spirit to work the life of my Son and my will through you.

----o----

What shall we say, then? Is the law sinful? Certainly not! Nevertheless, I would not have known what sin was had it not been for the law. For I would not have known what coveting really was if the law had not said, "You shall not covet." [8] But sin, seizing the opportunity afforded by the commandment, produced in me every kind of coveting. For apart from the law, sin was dead. Romans 7:7-8

"I am the vine; you are the branches. If you remain in me and I in you, you will bear much fruit; apart from me you can do nothing. John 15:5

46.

FREEDOM WITHOUT LAWLESSNESS

My Child . . .

Your freedom in my Son is not a license for you to live without restraint. You are not under the Law as you have died to the Law. But you are to live a life worthy of my Son. The Law did its job of showing you what sin is. This led to your realising you needed a solution for your sin. This in turn led you to my Son as your Saviour. So the Law remains to do its work in the life of those who don't know my Son. You are now 'born again.' So now it's not a case of you trying to keep the Law but for you to come under authority. Your freedom from the Law and the sin nature now means you are answerable to someone over you. Your real freedom comes when you submit to the Holy Spirit to work in your life. Moment-by-moment trusting in the indwelling Holy Spirit to control your life. Holy Spirit will empower you to live for my Son. Measure your life against how you follow the leading of the Holy Spirit.

----o----

But if you are led by the Spirit, you are not under the law. Galatians 5:18

----o----

So I say, walk by the Spirit, and you will not gratify the desires of the flesh. Galatians 5:16

----o----

47.

ULTIMATE FREEDOM

My Child . . .

Do you remember the Tabernacle and The Temple. One day per year, the Day of Atonement, the High Priest went into the Holy of Holies. He sprinkled the blood of an animal sacrifice onto the Mercy Seat. He was the High Priest and the only person allowed to go beyond the curtain on that one day. But remember what happened when my Son died on the cross. The Veil in the temple tore in two. Torn from top to bottom. My Son became your High Priest and opened the way to the Holy of Holies for you by His blood once for all time. But you don't need to go to a tabernacle or a temple. The way to me is open through my Son. This is the ultimate freedom my Son has won for you.

Through my Son you can come into my presence. The blood was sprinkled on the Mercy Seat, and above that Mercy Seat between the cherubim is where I dwelt on earth. Now the blood of my Son gives you total freedom to me. This is a freedom like no freedom before it. I want you to experience it. Come to me at any time. Approach me and dwell in my presence. I have an open-door policy with my children The door to me is never closed. You have to take hold of this freedom and live it. You can close your door of openness to me. When you do I am knocking on your door.

----o----

There, above the cover between the two cherubim that are over the ark of the covenant law, I will meet with you and give you all my commands for the Israelites. Exodus 25:22

----o----

In him and through faith in him we may approach God with freedom and confidence. Ephesians 3:12

48.

GUILT TRIPS

My Child . . .

Do not allow yourself to accept guilt for that which you are not guilty of. When you sin you are guilty for that sin. And we deal with that through confession, repentance, and forgiveness. Satan will try to impose guilt on you that you do not have to bear. He will remind you of things you have done wrong in your past and aim to make you feel guilty about them. I'm speaking of things that I have already forgiven you for and that you have moved on from. You will know it's not me speaking to you because I will not pour guilt on you or accuse you. Remember, there is no condemnation from me to you. Satan condemns. Whenever you 'feel' guilty try and examine yourself to see what you mean.

Are you guilty of a crime? Or are you having feelings of remorse because you think you could have done better? Guilty can weigh you down and bring depression. My Son has dealt with guilt for you. You do not have to wallow in guilt. You do not have to wallow in condemnation. Freedom from guilt is a victory won by my Son. When you do experience true guilt for your actions, deal with it the proper way. Oh yes, and don't feel guilty for the blessings I give you because you don't see others getting those blessings. Always rejoice in my gifts to you.

----o----

My guilt has overwhelmed me like a burden too heavy to bear. Psalm 38:4

----o----

"'These are the regulations for the guilt offering, which is most holy: The guilt offering is to be slaughtered in the place where the burnt offering is slaughtered, and its blood is to be splashed against the sides of the altar. Leviticus 7:1-2

----o----

let us draw near to God with a sincere heart and with the full assurance that faith brings, having our hearts sprinkled to cleanse us from a guilty conscience and having our bodies washed with pure water. Hebrews 10:22

49.

FREEDOM TO SERVE

My Child . . .

You were once a slave to your sin nature, the Law, and the Devil. But you are no longer a slave to them. You have been purchased at an incredibly high price. The death of my Son. No one else could have set you free from such slavery. No one else could set you free at no cost to yourself. So now you have a choice. Imagine if a person purchased a slave from a slave trader. The slave would have to do the bidding of their new owner. Imagine though if the buyer turned around and told the slave they were now free to go. No obligation to the buyer. No more forced labour for the buyer. Free to go where they wanted and live how they wanted. How might they then feel towards the buyer?

This is what my Son has done for you. He has paid the price and set you free. Based on this act of mercy towards you, what might be a suitable response to my Son. The only reasonable thing to do is to become a servant of my Son. Use your freedom to serve.

----o----

Therefore, I urge you, brothers and sisters, in view of God's mercy, to offer your bodies as a living sacrifice, holy and pleasing to God—this is your true and proper worship. Romans 12:1

----o----

50.

REGENERATE

My Child . . .

You have been 'born again' which means you have received Holy Spirit into your life. The instant you put your trust in the death of my Son for your sins you were sealed with the Spirit. This means the Spirit will never leave you. Holy Spirit has entered your life to regenerate your life. To make you a new person. Learn and understand the way the Spirit is working within you. Gain an understanding of His leading. He will guide you to places you would never have thought of going by yourself. He will lead you to places of ministry. He will lead you to deep healing. He has a gift for you to serve the body of Christ with. He will guide, comfort and encourage you. He will be like the wind blowing where it wants without being seen. But though the Spirit cannot be seen His presence is recognised by the way you live. The most important work of the Holy Spirit in your life is to transform you into the image of my Son. You are to be light in the world and you can only be that light by the power of the Holy Spirit. The cross has made your regeneration possible. There was no other way.

----o----

You should not be surprised at my saying, 'You must be born again.' [8] The wind blows wherever it pleases. You hear its sound, but you cannot tell where it comes from or where it is going. So it is with everyone born of the Spirit. John 3:7-8

----o----

I want to know Christ—yes, to know the power of his resurrection and participation in his sufferings, becoming like him in his death, Philippians 3:10

----o----

When Jesus spoke again to the people, he said, "I am the light of the world. Whoever follows me will never walk in darkness, but will have the light of life." John 8:12

51.

LISTENING RENOVATION

My Child . . .

Being 'born again' has brought you into my family. But this is not the end of your Spiritual journey. It is not a case of being Spiritually reborn and waiting until you die and then you are with me. I have called you to fellowship with my Son and I. My Son wants to renovate your life in his image. He does this via the Holy Spirit. Holy Spirit is the power source for your Spiritual walk. He renovates according to your openness to receive what he has for you. He will not force himself upon you. He will wait for you to invite him to have fellowship. It's a question of your will. It's your choice. My Son has provided the way for you to come close. We were separated but the cross has brought us together. Listen for my Son speaking to you by the Holy Spirit. It may not be a loud voice. You need to learn to listen carefully. Listen for that still small voice. You will know it when you hear it. It will not necessarily be audible. But in your inner ' born again' self you will know the voice when it speaks to you. This calls you to be still and take time to seek my will.

----o----

He says, "Be still, and know that I am God, Psalm 46:10a

----o----

Here I am! I stand at the door and knock. If anyone hears my voice and opens the door, I will come in and eat with that person, and they with me. Revelation 3:20

----o----

52.

POINTS OF VIEW

My Child . . .

You are able to see things from two points of view. You know how to see things from the point of view of a natural person without the Holy Spirit. You are also able to see things from the point of view of being 'born again' by the Spirit. This can be conflicting for you. On many occasions these points of view can be at enmity with each other. The natural point of view makes you see things with the sense that you are in control of your life. The Spiritual point of view reminds you that your life is in my Son's hands and my will is to be done. Though this conflict is difficult for you I allow it so that you can be sure what choice you are making. I want to encourage you that when you listen to Holy Spirit, and follow His direction, your life will be in its best place. It may not mean that you have a life of ease and leisure. It may mean you face suffering. The good thing is that it will mean the avenues of your life will work together for good. In the most difficult of circumstances you will be able to find peace and calm. In fact my peace will work to guide you. Chose the point of view you want to dominate your life. Allow Holy Spirit to guide your natural life day by day.

----o----

And we know that in all things God works for the good of those who love him, who have been called according to his purpose. Romans 8:28

----o----

May the God of hope fill you with all joy and peace as you trust in him, so that you may overflow with hope by the power of the Holy Spirit. Romans 15:13

53.

FAITH INTIMACY

My Child . . .

It's by faith that you grow in intimacy with me. Faith is reliant on me to be faithful to you. I am able. Believe always that I am able. For your faith to be effective you must believe that I can do what I say I can do. You don't need to pray for more faith. You have all the faith you need. Your faith needs an object to focus on. For you that means to focus on my Son. My blessings are available in him. He is the focus for your life. If you feel my Son is distant then read my Word to find him there. Learn of him. As you read my word you will discover things to believe. Things to put your faith in. As your understanding of my Son and what he has done for you grows, so will your faith in him. Holy Spirit will help you with this. You will learn to believe more. You will learn to believe in things that you cannot see with your natural eyes. You will find intimacy with Father, Son and Holy Spirit, greater than you have known before. Increasingly so.

----o----

Now faith is confidence in what we hope for and assurance about what we do not see. Hebrew 11:1

----o----

Fixing our eyes on Jesus, the pioneer and perfecter of faith. For the joy set before him he endured the cross, scorning its shame, and sat down at the right hand of the throne of God. Hebrews 12:2

----o----

54.

SELF-CENTRED TO CHRIST-CENTRED

My Child . . .

Be very clear that your flesh is your enemy. Your flesh is that part of you that wants to control your life rather than being led by the Holy Spirit. The flesh will be seen in your attitudes and reasons that you live the way you do. Because of the victory my Son has won through the cross you can now put off the old person and put on the new. Live to overcome the flesh by the Spirit. Set you mind now on things from above and not on the things of this world. Believe the fact that you have died to the flesh and to the things of the world. You may or may not be experiencing your new found life through the work of the cross. Believe though that it is a reality. I see the new you! In the unsaved, self-centredness is a primary concern. That is what the self considers important. In the new you, Christ centredness is to be your primary concern. Pleasing and serving him becomes your focus. Believe the old you is crucified with Christ. Believe the new you is resurrected with him. This is the way to living a Christian life. Be centred on my Son, not yourself.

Therefore, if anyone is in Christ, the new creation has come: The old has gone, the new is here! 2 Corinthians 5:17

Since, then, you have been raised with Christ, set your hearts on things above, where Christ is, seated at the right hand of God. ² Set your minds on things above, not on earthly things. ³ For you died, and your life is now hidden with Christ in God. Colossians 3:1-3

55.

CLAIM THE VICTORY

My Child . . .

My Son has won the victory for you. What he accomplished at the cross is the mystery that people have waited many years for. And still some don't see it. The cross has made it possible for your life to be transformed. The victory my Son has won for you is a victory you have to claim. You need to stand in that victory. Believe in the victory. This is your responsibility. You are responsible to choose to follow my ways. Seeking my will is a responsibility you are never free from. You can choose not to seek my will but that does not stop the fact that you should be seeking my will. The power to live for me is the power of the Holy Spirit. It is not of yourself. The power will come when you obey my Word. Obedience is what I look for. Not in the sense of you trying to keep the Law. But from a heart that desires to serve me because it recognises the great salvation it has gained. A costly salvation through the blood of my Son. Don't look for power. Don't want the victory at no cost to yourself. When you obey you show where your heart is looking. Seek and obey with all your heart and the victory of the cross will bear fruit in your life.

----o----

But Samuel replied: "Does the Lord delight in burnt offerings and sacrifices as much as in obeying the Lord? To obey is better than sacrifice, and to heed is better than the fat of rams. 1Samuel 15:22

----o----

for it is God who works in you to will and to act in order to fulfill his good purpose. Philippians 2:13

56.

BEST PLAN

My Child . . .

My plan for your life is the best plan for your life. My Son lived, died, and was resurrected so we could be reconciled. So you could be transformed. Believe that my plan is the best for you. As you are changed you will discover what I have called you to be and do. There will also be things I call you to stop doing. Because I love you my plan is the highest plan for your life. The transformation that I bring into your life will make your life the best it can be. Remember that what I call you to do I also provide the power for you to do it. Holy Spirit is the power in your life. So you do not have to worry. I will remain faithful to you in all things. I will always be there for you. Holy Spirit will always be within you. My Son will always make intercession for you. But we will not force ourselves upon you. You will always have free will. Holy Spirit will speak into your life but you need to be ready to take action. You can't steer a car unless it's moving. The Holy Spirit can't steer your life if you don't step out in obedience to what he says. Be ready to move.

----o----

In a large house there are articles not only of gold and silver, but also of wood and clay; some are for special purposes and some for common use. [21] Those who cleanse themselves from the latter will be instruments for special purposes, made holy, useful to the Master and prepared to do any good work. 2 Timothy 2:20-21

----o----

57.

BEAR FRUIT

My Child . . .

Always ask the Holy Spirit to search you, cleanse you, and renew you. Don't live your life as an ordinary person does as if the Holy Spirit is not in you. You are no longer an ordinary person. You have believed in the victory of the cross and have abundant life available to you. You can either live by walking in the Spirit or you can live by letting your old nature control you. Either will be shown by the way you live. Your life will either show the fruits of the Spirit or the fruits of the flesh. Maybe a combination of both as the Spirit works a transformation within you. Your aim should be to bear the fruits of the Spirit. This is what pleases me and my Son. You cannot bear fruit by yourself. Without my Son you can do nothing. The Spirit will only speak to you what he hears from my Son. All that is mine is available in my Son. The Spirit will receive from my Son and make it known unto you. Understand this. All of mine is available to my Son who will impart things to you via the Holy Spirit. Bring all of your life under the authority of the Son by the power of the Holy Spirit.

----o----

Brothers and sisters, I could not address you as people who live by the Spirit but as people who are still worldly—mere infants in Christ. [2] I gave you milk, not solid food, for you were not yet ready for it. Indeed, you are still not ready. [3] You are still worldly. For since there is jealousy and quarreling among you, are you not worldly? Are you not acting like mere humans? 1 Corinthians 3:1-3

----o----

I am the vine; you are the branches. If you remain in me and I in you, you will bear much fruit; apart from me you can do nothing. John 15:5

----o----

But when he, the Spirit of truth, comes, he will guide you into all the truth. He will not speak on his own; he will speak only what he hears, and he will tell you what is yet to come. John 16:13

----o----

All that belongs to the Father is mine. That is why I said the Spirit will receive from me what he will make known to you. John 16:15

----o----

58.

NEW POSITION

My Child . . .

Do you want to be a mature Christian? The only way to live in a deeper Spirituality is through the cross. The way to power and victory is to understand and live in the new position my Son has won for you. People have called it by different names. Some call it, Baptised in the Holy Spirit. Others, a Spirit filled life. Still others, a higher life or crucified life. Whatever people want to call it, it is only available through the cross. You may look for it through service. You may use biblical meditation, books, spiritual teachings and many other well-meaning methods. But it can only be found through my Son. Through my Son and what he accomplished by the cross. You must stand in your new position in my Son. To me, you are one with my Son. I totally see you in my Son. Imagine if a glass of fresh drinking water was poured into the sea. Immediately the fresh water is consumed by the salty sea and becomes one with the ocean. This is how fully you are one with my Son. If you want a deeper spiritual life abide in him. He is the door to life abundantly.

----o----

[9] For in Christ all the fullness of the Deity lives in bodily form, [10] and in Christ you have been brought to fullness. He is the head over every power and authority. Colossians 2:9-10

----o----

59.

BLESSINGS

My Child . . .

Because of the cross you have received multiple blessings. These are blessings that cannot be earned but are freely given to you once you enter into salvation. The are yours when you are 'in Christ' my Son. These blessings are not only for your life here on earth. They are yours for eternity. These eternal blessings are worth much more than temporary material earthly blessings. Your Spiritual blessings include, forgiveness, freedom, righteousness, redemption, to but name a few. I want you to begin living now in your eternal Spiritual blessings. I want you to explore my Word and find all the blessings that you are now blessed with. Remember that positionally you are in Christ and all the blessings are yours. Experientially you are in the process of regeneration. You have to learn to live out the blessings in your day-to-day life. This is why I keep reminding you to 'walk in the Spirit' each day.

----o----

[3] Praise be to the God and Father of our Lord Jesus Christ, who has blessed us in the heavenly realms with every spiritual blessing in Christ. Ephesians 1:3

----o----

[16] So I say, walk by the Spirit, Galatians 5:16a

----o----

60.

ONENESS

My Child . . .

Because of the cross you have entered into oneness with my Son. You have become a part of his body. His body is the Church. You are to live in union with him. Just as a man and woman become husband and wife and live life together as one, so you are called to live as one with my Son. To live in oneness. This oneness is yours when you believe. That is your position in my Son. Live reflecting that oneness. In all your life journey in prayer and obedience to the work of the Holy Spirit. Holy Spirit will equip you to live the Christian life. There is no other way you can live it. It is not easy to make your position your experience. This is why you need to learn of me and my Son. Learn of all that we have done for you. Gain an understanding of our nature and how much we love you. Read my Word and see the magnificent future I have for you, both in this life and in your life after death. See the hope that is in myself, my Son and my Word. Believe in faith in the hope you see. Seek my will. Ask Holy Spirit to reveal my things to you. Especially the oneness you have in my Son.

----o----

After all, no one ever hated their own body, but they feed and care for their body, just as Christ does the church— 30 for we are members of his body. 31 "For this reason a man will leave his father and mother and be united to his wife, and the two will become one flesh." 32 This is a profound mystery—but I am talking about Christ and the church.

61.

SPIRITUAL BANKRUPT

My Child . . .

Don't live like a Spiritual bankrupt. I have great riches for you. Live in them. Your salvation is not a case of waiting until you die and then you get the benefits. The benefits of your salvation start immediately. Claim them! Live them! Don't live in Spiritual poverty. Learn of how the victory of the cross can be implemented in your life on a daily basis. Live in the riches of my grace. I can do abundantly above all you can ask or think. This is because of the cross. What a victory available to you! Believe me when I tell you this. You live believing that my Son died for your sin and that you are born-again. And so you should. Don't be unbelieving of all else that has been won for you. You are now identified in my

Son's death, burial, and resurrection. You have the antidote for overcoming sin. It's this victory over sin that prevents you from being helpless. In your struggles against the world, the flesh, and the Devil you have a road to victory. You have a complete salvation. Claim it.

----o----

But thanks be to God! He gives us the victory through our Lord Jesus Christ.

1 Corinthians 15:57

----o----

Then Jesus said to his disciples, "Whoever wants to be my disciple must deny themselves and take up their cross and follow me. Matthew 16:24

----o----

And having disarmed the powers and authorities, he made a public spectacle of them, triumphing over them by the cross. Colossians 2:15

----o----

"He himself bore our sins" in his body on the cross, so that we might die to sins and live for righteousness; "by his wounds you have been healed." 1 Peter 2:24

62.

ADAM TO CHRIST

My Child . . .

My Son the Last Adam. The first Adam got people into a tragic disorder by introducing sin into the world. But the mess that the first Adam got people into, the Last Adam, my Son, provides people a way out. You were born into union with the first Adam and you inherited the sin nature. Now, by being born-again, you are born into union with Jesus my Son. You are now dead to sin and alive to Christ. Your old life was identified with the first Adam. Your new life is to be lived identified with my Son. You are crucified with Christ. Learn of my Son and his victory over sin at the cross and how it now applies to you. In the first Adam you were dead in sin. Since you have died and been resurrected in my Son, you are now to consider yourself dead to sin and alive to him. Walk in such a way as to put to death the deeds of the sinful nature. Put off the old self and put on the new self. Be renewed in the understanding and image of my Son.

----o----

For if, by the trespass of the one man, death reigned through that one man, how much more will those who receive God's abundant provision of grace and of the gift of righteousness reign in life through the one man, Jesus Christ! Romans 5:17

----o----

Since, then, you have been raised with Christ, set your hearts on things above, where Christ is, seated at the right hand of God. [2] Set your minds on things above, not on earthly things. Colossians 3:1-2

63.

DON'T PUNISH YOURSELF

My Child . . .

When you sin don't spend your time punishing yourself. The punishment for your sin has already been taken. When you sin don't wallow in feeling guilty. The guilt has already been paid for. I want you to realise that when you sin you need to turn to the solution for that sin. Because of the cross the solution for you is confession and asking forgiveness. It is of no benefit to wallow in your failure or to think that by punishing yourself you make everything fine. It's only the blood of my Son that deals with your sin. Make this a reality in your life by recognising you are dead to sin and as a fact receive it by faith in my Son. Seek for my Son to live his life through you. You will not find any shortcuts to Spiritual maturity. You are not instantly perfect in the way you live. Your Spiritual life in my Son begins as if you are a baby and little by little you grow into adulthood. That journey cannot be taken in your own strength. Don't punish yourself and live in discouragement and failure. Yield yourself to my Son and allow Holy Spirit to work in you.

----o----

"For through the law I died to the law so that I might live for God. [20] I have been crucified with Christ and I no longer live, but Christ lives in me. The life I now live in the body, I live by faith in the Son of God, who loved me and gave himself for me. [21] I do not set aside the grace of God, for if righteousness could be gained through the law, Christ died for nothing!" Galatians 2:19-20

64.

FOCUS ON THE SON NOT SIN

My Child . . .

Live being 'Son' conscious. Don't focus your life on your sins. Focus rather on the fact of my Son's forgiveness. In other words, don't be sin conscious, but rather be 'Son' conscious. If you focus on your sin you will end up condemning yourself. Then you might try to use your own effort to overcome your sin. That will never work for you. Think of my Son and not sin. Thinking of my Son can remind you of our love and unconditional acceptance of you. It can remind you of the forgiveness won for you on the cross. It's best for you not to focus on the problem but on the problem solver. All my children have issues in their life that they would like me to change. Change will happen for you when you focus more on the Change Maker than on what you want to see changed. When you become conscious of your sin run headlong into my forgiveness and faithfulness. Read my Word. Get my Word into your mind and heart. Put to death the old-self by the renewing of your mind. As your new ways of thinking begin to take hold you will little by little take on the new-person you are in Christ.

----o----

How can a young person stay on the path of purity? By living according to your word. 10 I seek you with all my heart; do not let me stray from your commands. 11 I have hidden your word in my heart that I might not sin against you. Psalm 119:9-11

----o----

Do not conform to the pattern of this world, but be transformed by the renewing of your mind. Then you will be able to test and approve what God's will is—his good, pleasing and perfect will. Romans 12:2

65.

UNWORTHY

My Child . . .

It is not Spiritual to feel unworthy. Some live their life looking down on themselves as being worthless and unusable for service to me. That is very far from the truth. You are made worthy by my Son and what he has achieved for you. You have been lifted to an exalted position in my Son. You don't have to earn my love and acceptance because that is a given for you. Don't focus any longer on the old person you were but rather focus on your new self-image in my Son. I think of you very highly. You are precious to me. It is not simply a case of who you are but now a case of Whose you are. You are mine and no one can snatch you out of my hand. See yourself in a whole new light because of being in my Son. My Son is the King of Kings and that means you are now royalty. Royalty in my kingdom. You are chosen, holy, and a royal priest. You are my precious possession. I have taken you out of darkness into my wonderful light. Walk in the light. Declare my praises!

----o----

But you are a chosen people, a royal priesthood, a holy nation, God's special possession, that you may declare the praises of him who called you out of darkness into his wonderful light. 1 Peter 2:9

----o----

but those who hope in the Lord will renew their strength. They will soar on wings like eagles; they will run and not grow weary, they will walk and not be faint. Isaiah 40:31

66.

BEAUTIFUL FEET

My Child . . .

Love sent my Son to the cross. He did not die only for those who would believe in him. He died also for all those who would reject him. He died for those who despised him. He died for those who caused him great sorrow. He went to the depths of grief for all the world. He was ridiculed. His salvation was ignored by most. His words were received by few. His authority was seldom accepted. ignored. Yet the whole world can be saved because he endured the cross. He did not go to the cross because the world wanted him to. He went to the cross because of his great love for me and for the world. He wanted to make reconciliation to me an option for all people. And that is what he has done. The message of salvation is for all people. But how will people hear the message if no one tells them? And if they don't hear the message how can people gain salvation? The cross is for the whole world but only effective for those who trust in it. Tell the message. Declare the truth. Sow seeds for salvation.

----o----

How beautiful on the mountains are the feet of those who bring good news, who proclaim peace, who bring good tidings, who proclaim salvation, who say to Zion, "Your God reigns!" Isaiah 52:7

67.

ACCEPTED OR REJECTED

My Child . . .

Remember that a gift can be offered to a person but until they take the gift it is not theirs. So it is with the gift of salvation my Son offers. It is possible for everyone in the whole world to be saved if they take the gift offered to them. It is their freewill choice to accept or reject the free gift. They can accept or reject my Son dying on their behalf instead of them. They can believe my Son is the only mediator between themselves and I, if they want to. They can choose to accept that their debt of sin is paid in full. And they can choose to want to be reconciled to me believing that is only possible through my Son. Remember too that Satan will seek to blind your listeners to this good news. The pull of the world and not wanting to let go of what they have will hold them back from committing to my Son. There will be many and varied reasons to reject the gift. Do not let that dismay you from sharing the gift is available. You are not responsible for the decisions of others. But you are responsible to live in the light and to be ready to give an account of what you believe. Let your light shine!

In the same way, let your light shine before others, that they may see your good deeds and glorify your Father in heaven. Matthew 5:16

And the Lord's servant must not be quarrelsome but must be kind to everyone, able to teach, not resentful. [25] Opponents must be gently instructed, in the hope that God will grant them repentance leading them to a knowledge of the truth, ²⁶ and that they will come to their senses and escape from the trap of the devil, who has taken them captive to do his will. 2 Timothy 2:24-26

68.

DO NOT ADD OR TAKE AWAY

My Child . . .

Don't make the results of salvation the means of attaining salvation. There is a difference between how you gained your salvation and the results of it in your life. There is no quality of life that you have achieved that has helped you attain salvation. Salvation is a free gift. As such, if any work is done to achieve it then it no longer remains a free gift but a result of works. It cannot be attained by any work that seeks to earn salvation. My redemptive plan stands alone. There is nothing to be added to it and there is nothing to be taken away from it. It is the plan of redemption that can only be received by faith and not by works. It is by my grace that you or anyone else can receive salvation.

Therefore, do not add anything to the salvation message and do not take anything away from the salvation message. Declare Christ crucified for the sins of the world and that salvation is in no other. Trust Holy Spirit to speak to people's hearts as you share this important truth with them.

----o----

For it is by grace you have been saved, through faith—and this is not from yourselves, it is the gift of God— [9] not by works, so that no one can boast. Ephesians 2:8-9

----o----

69.

CHEAP GRACE?

My Child . . .

My grace means I give to people freely that which they cannot deserve or earn in any way by their own efforts. You have no reason to boast of how you gained your salvation. You have no reason to take pride in achieving reconciliation with me. All that has been achieved for you through the cross is available at no cost to you. Purely given by my grace towards you. Do not consider because I give freely that it has not come at a high cost. It is not cheap grace. It is grace won for you by my son at the cross. It cost my son his life. Think about this. In your natural world what could you pay a loving father for the life of their son? A true loving father would not accept any fee in exchange for the life of their son. It was only because of our great love for you that my Son was allowed to pay the price that no one else could possibly pay. Accept all I offer with a thankful heart knowing that you could not have earned any of it. Accept it knowing it is given in love and acceptance to you my child.

----o----

And if by grace, then it cannot be based on works; if it were, grace would no longer be grace. Romans 11:6

70.

FAITH RESPONSE

My Child . . .

It would probably make you feel happy if a person came to you and said they have a gift for you. But you might then feel immediately unhappy if the person said you could only have the gift if you did some work for it. If you have to work for a gift then it is no longer a gift. If you work for something, whatever is received in recompense for that work is in effect wages. This is why your salvation is received by faith. Faith is the belief in something that you cannot see. All you have to do is believe in something you cannot see. In this case it is the fact that my Son died on the cross for your sins. This is not a work to earn salvation. It's simply choosing that which you choose to believe. You put your faith in my Son and he puts his righteousness into you.

----o----

Now faith is confidence in what we hope for and assurance about what we do not see. Hebrews 11:1

----o----

Now to the one who works, wages are not credited as a gift but as an obligation. [5] However, to the one who does not work but trusts God who justifies the ungodly, their faith is credited as righteousness. Romans 4:4-5

----o----

71.

FAITH PLUS REPENTANCE?

My Child . . .

Repentance calls a person to a change of mind and direction. Some would say a person needs to repent first and then put faith in my Son. Having heard the message of salvation for their sins, a person who believes has in fact repented. Their mind has been changed and they have turned to my Son for forgiveness. The danger with repentance is that some people think it should be shown by an act of penitence shown by tears and deep groanings of remorse. Those things may happen for some people. They are not a prerequisite for believing unto salvation. Do not declare the gospel and seek an emotional response for sin from people. Declare the gospel and encourage people to believe the good news. To believe it sincerely and to pray and ask my Son for forgiveness. My word speaks to the mind and to the heart. My word is objective truth and requires only a mental choice to accept it's truth. Then a person needs to put faith in that truth. So don't add repentance as an act of contrition that must take place before a person believes. Emotions may be involved when a person believes, but it is the acceptance of the truth by faith that matters. Yes, call people to repentance and to believe. Don't call them to emotional experiences as proof of their sincerity.

----o----

"........[3] I tell you, no! But unless you repent, you too will all perish. [4] Or those eighteen who died when the tower in Siloam fell on them—do you think they were more guilty than all the others living in Jerusalem? [5] I tell you, no! But unless you repent, you too will all perish." Luke 13:3-5

----o----

Repent, then, and turn to God, so that your sins may be wiped out, that times of refreshing may come from the Lord, Acts 3:19

72.

FAITH PLUS BAPTISM?

My Child . . .

Always remember that baptism is a result of salvation and not part of the cause of salvation. Never add baptism as a prerequisite to gaining salvation. It is not a stipulation to get saved. You are saved by faith alone. Though I call people to water baptism it is not a ritual to add to faith for salvation. The same way the early church was not to add circumcision to faith so you must not add baptism to faith. Abraham believed me and it was counted to him as righteousness in my sight. Later came his circumcision. It was the outward sign of the seal of the faith he had while still uncircumcised. Anything added to faith for salvation is based on human merit. This is irreconcilable with my grace.

Though Paul the Apostle did baptise some believers, I did not send him to baptise. I sent him to preach the gospel. When a person believes the good news it is my power that brings salvation.

----o----

If, in fact, Abraham was justified by works, he had something to boast about—but not before God. ³ What does Scripture say? "Abraham believed God, and it was credited to him as righteousness." Romans 4:2-3

----o----

For Christ did not send me to baptize, but to preach the gospel—not with wisdom and eloquence, lest the cross of Christ be emptied of its power. 1 Corinthians 1:17

----o----

For I am not ashamed of the gospel, because it is the power of God that brings salvation to everyone who believes: first to the Jew, then to the Gentile. Romans 1:16

73.

CROSS OF PARADISE

My Child . . .

As my Son was being crucified he spoke to the thief on the cross. As he was dying the thief believed in my Son. The thief did not understand all the theology of the cross. What the thief did was to put faith in my Son. My Son told the thief he would be with him in paradise later that day. My Son didn't tell the thief to get down from the cross and go and do some good works before he died. He didn't tell him he would miss out on paradise because he did not have time to get baptized. He didn't tell him to evangelise or live a holy life to prove his beliefs. Yes, there will be good deeds of various kinds to follow salvation. But the thief on the cross shows that a person's own human effort has no claim on achieving salvation. If I can save a thief on a cross by faith alone then I can do that for everyone who believes. And indeed I do!

----o----

[39] One of the criminals who hung there hurled insults at him: "Aren't you the Messiah? Save yourself and us!" [40] But the other criminal rebuked him. "Don't you fear God," he said, "since you are under the same sentence? [41] We are punished justly, for we are getting what our deeds deserve. But this man has done nothing wrong." [42] Then he said, "Jesus, remember me when you come into your kingdom." [43] Jesus answered him, "Truly I tell you, today you will be with me in paradise." Luke 23:39-43

----o----

74.

TAKE UP YOUR CROSS

My Child . . .

You are called to take up your cross. You cannot bear the cross for the sins of the world as my Son did. That would not be possible neither is it required. But you are called to bear your own cross and follow my Son. My Son must be your first love. You can love all others as deeply as you can but not more than you love my Son. This is so you can follow my Son where ever he calls you. If you love others more than Him you will not be fully sold out for my Son. You run the risk of following what they want instead of my Son's call on your life. Don't make your way in this world at the expense of serving my Son. You will find a form of life so much less than what my Son has available to you. Follow my Son by denying your life in this world and you will find a greater life both in this world and the next. Seek first the kingdom of God. Seek my Son with all your heart. If the way you live is no different to a non-Christian then you need to ask yourself if you are carrying your cross. Live a life worthy of a Saviour who pursued and carried His cross for you.

----o----

"Anyone who loves their father or mother more than me is not worthy of me; anyone who loves their son or daughter more than me is not worthy of me. 38 Whoever does not take up their cross and follow me is not worthy of me. 39 Whoever finds their life will lose it, and whoever loses their life for my sake will find it. Matthew 10:38

----o----

75.

MISUNDERSTOOD CROSS

My Child . . .

The cross was confusing to many. Even to those who were well versed in the scriptures. The chief priests and the teachers of the law did not recognise that my Son was the Messiah. They had not understood the prophecies. They were looking for a different sort of Messiah. They wanted a conquering Messiah not a suffering servant. If they had understood the cross they would not have mocked him. If they had understood they would not have said that if he was the king he should come down from the cross. They did not believe he was my Son and implied if he was I should rescue him. But my Son chose the cross. He chose to die for those who despised and rejected him. It was not for me to rescue him from pouring out his love in this way. Without the cross the creation was lost to me and I to the creation. There are still those today who say if my Son was the Son of God then he would have come down from the cross. They too do not understand the cross and why my Son did not deliver himself from it. It was love that held him on that cross. What is seen by so many as a defeat for my Son was in fact the greatest victory the creation has ever known.

----o----

⁴¹ In the same way the chief priests, the teachers of the law and the elders mocked him. ⁴² "He saved others," they said, "but he can't save himself! He's the king of Israel! Let him come down now from the cross, and we will believe in him. ⁴³ He trusts in God. Let God rescue him now if he wants him, for he said, 'I am the Son of God.'" Matthew 27:41-43

----o----

76.

CROSS OF POWER

AND WISDOM

My Child . . .

Sadly, to those who will not believe, the cross is seen as foolish and irrelevant. For many various reasons the cross is rejected by many. When the cross is rejected then my Son and I are rejected. Salvation is rejected. Those who believe it is foolish are those that are perishing. But the message of the cross is not foolish. To you who is saved the cross is my power in your life. It is my wisdom in your life. Some look for signs. What a sign the cross is and yet people miss it. But it's not the type of sign they are looking for. They want signs so they do not have to use their faith. They can only be saved through faith. Others look for wisdom. They want to be able to understand and explain things with their intellect. But they can never by mere human intellect understand the deep mystery of the cross. It can only be understood by faith. The mystery of the cross is my wisdom. Its message needs to be received and believed. I do not look for you to understand everything. That is impossible for you. I look to you to believe what I reveal to you and put your faith in it. Don't look for a sign. Don't seek to fully comprehend. Don't stop believing.

----o----

[18] For the message of the cross is foolishness to those who are perishing, but to us who are being saved it is the power of God............ [22] Jews demand signs and Greeks look for wisdom, [23] but we preach Christ crucified: a stumbling block to Jews and foolishness to Gentiles, [24] but to those whom God has called, both

Jews and Greeks, Christ the power of God and the wisdom of God. ²⁵ For the foolishness of God is wiser than human wisdom, and the weakness of God is stronger than human strength. 1 Corinthians 1:18, 22-25

77.

WHO PUT MY SON ON THE CROSS?

My Child . . .

Do not think there is ever a time when I am not in control of the outcome of what happens in your world. Never think that the death of my Son took me by surprise. Don't consider for one moment that I could not have sent thousands upon thousands of angels to rescue my Son. His death was my plan for my reconciliation to my creation. People took him and put him on the cross. They let him die like a common criminal. Ultimately his death was my will. Wicked men tortured him and mocked him. His own people cried out for him to be crucified. He was scourged and nailed to death. And yet is was my will for him to die. But more profound is the fact that my Son willingly endured such a death for you. His death is personal for you. How personal is his death for you? Have you ever asked yourself who put my Son on the cross? The answer is exactly why the death of my Son is personal to you. Who put my Son on the cross? You did. Your sin put my Son on the cross. Be assured if you were the only person who had ever sinned my son would have died for you. This is how much he loves you.

----o----

This man was handed over to you by God's deliberate plan and foreknowledge; and you, with the help of wicked men, put him to death by nailing him to the cross. Acts:2:23

----o----

78.

DON'T BE AN ENEMY

OF THE CROSS

My Child . . .

To embrace the cross is to invite enemies. Not all want to hear the message of the cross. It's a message that cuts across a listener's self-reliance. Even some professing believes will not want you to rely solely on the cross. The would want you to perform some religious act to show your salvation and not want you to only put your faith in the work of the cross. They do not want to proclaim the cross because they know they will be persecuted for it. They are enemies of the cross. Don't you become any enemy of the cross. Never be ashamed of your wonderful Saviour. He was never ashamed to hang on the cross for you. Don't be embarrassed to tell of the cross when led to do so. It is the only thing that saves. It is the only work to put faith in for salvation through my Son.

---o----

Those who want to impress people by means of the flesh are trying to compel you to be circumcised. The only reason they do this is to avoid being persecuted for the cross of Christ. Galatians 6:12

----o----

For, as I have often told you before and now tell you again even with tears, many live as enemies of the cross of Christ. Philippians 3:18

----o----

79.

SET APART

My Child . . .

What do you boast about? No one has any reason to boast. All a person has is what I allow them to have. Yes, some have more than others. Some are poor in financial wealth but rich in Spiritual wealth. Some have abundant material possessions others few. There are those who have much who like to boast of all they have. There are some with very little and yet boast of how little they have. Some wealthy people think they can boast because in their mind their wealth is a sign of my blessing them. Others boast of how little they have because in their mind they think it makes them more humble than others. Remember that I allow it to rain on the rich and on the poor. What is important is not a matter of if you are rich or poor but who's will are you walking in? Are you walking in my will or your will? If you are going to boast then boast in the cross. You have been set apart by the cross. You are dead to the world. Don't live as if the things of the world are important to you. Don't live to increase your material wealth. Remember you have died with my Son and you're risen from death in my Son. Yes, live and work but make the goal and the desire of your heart to live for me. I will add to you all you need to walk in service to me. But not all your wants. Boast only in the cross and be set apart from the world.

----o----

May I never boast except in the cross of our Lord Jesus Christ, through which the world has been crucified to me, and I to the world. Galatians 6:14

----o----

80.

DON'T FORGET

My Child . . .

I want you to always remember the cross. Each day I want you to remember and be thankful for the cross and what my Son has done for you. That's why you are called to break bread and drink wine. To remember the cross. Remember that it's the body and the blood of my Son that is the only way into the new covenant. This is the message you are to proclaim to the unsaved. Never partake of the bread and the wine in a disrespectful way as that is a sin against the body and blood of my Son. Examine yourself before you partake of the bread and wine and approach it with humility and thanksgiving.

----o----

[23] For I received from the Lord what I also passed on to you: The Lord Jesus, on the night he was betrayed,

took bread,[24] and when he had given thanks, he broke it and said, "This is my body, which is for you; do this in remembrance of me. [25] In the same way, after supper he took the cup, saying, "This cup is the new covenant in my blood; do this, whenever you drink it, in remembrance of me." [26] For whenever you eat this bread and drink this cup, you proclaim the Lord's death until he comes.

[27] So then, whoever eats the bread or drinks the cup of the Lord in an unworthy manner will be guilty of sinning against the body and blood of the Lord. [28] Everyone ought to examine themselves before they eat of the bread and drink from the cup. 1 Corinthians 11:23-28

----o----

"MARANATHA!"

Come Lord Jesus!

Books by Paul

My Child Walk in the Spirit

My Child Your Father

My Child Survey the Wondrous Cross

In the Twinkling of an Eye

Living a Sheltered Life

4 Visions

www.ingramcontent.com/pod-product-compliance
Lightning Source LLC
Chambersburg PA
CBHW070535170426
43200CB00011B/2427